MW01538010

Original title: Spellcasters Tarot. Love, Money, Health, Protection, Success, and Beauty

© Spellcasters Tarot. Love, Money, Health, Protection, Success, and Beauty, Carlos Martínez Cerdá and Víctor Martínez Cerdá, 2025

Authors: Víctor Martínez Cerdá and Carlos Martínez Cerdá (V&C Brothers)

© Cover and illustrations: V&C Brothers

Layout and design: V&C Brothers

All rights reserved.

This publication may not be reproduced, stored, recorded, or transmitted in any form or by any means, whether mechanical, photochemical, electronic, magnetic, electro-optical, by photocopying, or information retrieval systems, or any other current or future method, without prior written permission from the copyright holders.

# SPELLCASTERS TAROT

Love, Money, Health, Protection, Success, and Beauty

"Magic is the art of transforming energy into reality."

# INDEX

## 9.8 Spell to Eliminate Insecurities About Physical Appearance

# 1
# MAGICAL PRECAUTIONS AND ETHICS

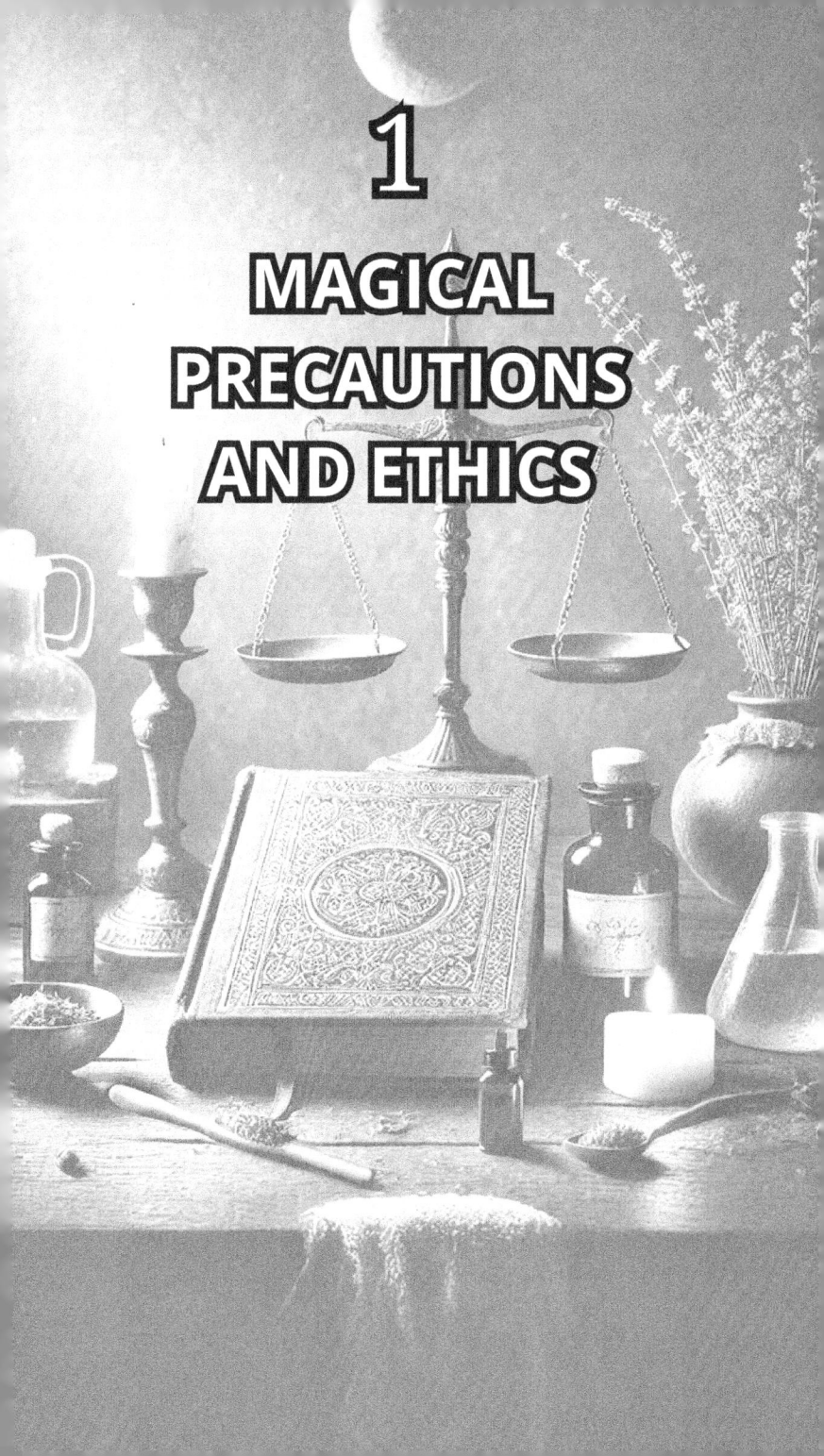

# 1

## Magical Precautions and Ethics

Magic is a powerful tool capable of influencing reality, but its use comes with great responsibility.

It should not be taken lightly, as every magical action generates effects that can manifest in different ways.

Before performing any ritual, it is essential to understand general precautions, ethical principles, and the possible repercussions of its practice.

Magic should be used with respect, awareness, and proper preparation.

## Precautions When Practicing Magic

### 1. Have a Clear and Defined Intention

-It is crucial to precisely define what you wish to manifest.

-Avoid vague or ambiguous desires, as energy will follow the direction you give it.

-Use clear and positive affirmations to avoid unexpected effects.

### 2. Energetic and Spiritual Protection

Before performing any spell, it is advisable to establish a protective barrier to prevent interference or unwanted energies:

-Cast a protective circle before starting any magical work.

-Carry protective stones such as obsidian, clear quartz, or black tourmaline.

-Visualize a white light surrounding you and purifying your energy.

-Burn herbs like sage, rue, or myrrh to cleanse the space.

-Take purification baths with sea salt and herbs before and after the ritual.

### 3. Do Not Rely Solely on Magic

-Magic is a supportive tool, not a substitute for personal effort.

-If you cast a spell for abundance or success, it is also necessary to take action in the physical world.

-Avoid seeing magic as a quick fix without working on internal and external changes.

Example: If you want to get a job through a spell, you should also send out résumés and prepare properly for interviews.

### 4. Caution with Manipulative Magic

-Spells intended to control another person's will can bring negative consequences.

-It is better to focus on attracting positive situations rather than directly influencing someone.

-Altering another's free will may generate negative karma or unexpected side effects.

Example: Instead of casting a spell for a specific person to fall in love with you, cast one to attract your ideal love, aligned with your well-being.

## 5. Keep Rituals Private

-Sharing too many details about your magical practices can weaken their effect.

-Other people's energy, doubts, or vibrations can interfere with your work.

-If you need to talk about it, do so only with trusted individuals who are knowledgeable about the subject.

### Ethics in Magic

### 1. The Law of Return

All energy you send out will return to you in some way.

-If you project love and good intentions, you will receive the same in return.

-If you use magic for destructive purposes, you may attract negative consequences.

Example: A revenge spell may backfire and affect your life in unexpected ways.

### 2. Do No Harm to Others

-Magic should be used for your own well-being and that of others, without causing harm or forcing situations.

-Avoid practices based on resentment, revenge, or selfishness.

### 3. Respect for Others' Free Will

-Manipulating someone else's thoughts, emotions, or decisions without their consent is unethical.

-This applies especially to love spells or mental control.

-If you wish to perform a ritual for someone else's benefit, ask for their permission first.

Golden Rule: Only perform spells for others if they give their approval.

## 4. Relationship with Spiritual Entities

-If you work with spirits, deities, or higher energies, do so with respect.

-Make offerings or give thanks when appropriate.

-Do not demand or command favors; instead, ask with humility.

-Always properly close any contact with spiritual beings after a ritual.

Example: If you invoke a deity's energy for protection, thank them with a symbolic gesture, such as a candle or a small offering.

## 5. Risks of Irresponsible Practice

Misusing magic can bring about undesired effects, such as:

-Negative Energy Return: Using magic with harmful intentions may attract adverse consequences.

-Emotional Imbalance: Practicing without mental stability can increase anxiety or cause exhaustion.

-Disconnection from Reality: Believing magic is the only solution to problems may lead to frustration.

-Attraction of Unwanted Energies: Invoking without proper

knowledge can attract undesired presences.

-Lack of Control: A poorly executed spell may produce unexpected results.

Example: If you perform a ritual to receive money without specifying the source, you might receive it in an unethical or unfavorable way.

## 6. Tips for Safe and Responsible Magical Practice

-Research before casting any spell. Do not engage in practices without understanding their purpose and effects.

-Follow your intuition. If something causes doubt or discomfort, it may not be the right time to proceed.

-Use magic as a complement, not the only solution.

-Protect your energy regularly. Perform spiritual cleansings and use protection methods.

-Respect nature and other people's beliefs. Everyone has their own spiritual path.

-Don't rush the results. Magic works at its own pace—be patient. If you have doubts about a spell's effectiveness or whether it's right to perform it, it's best to wait and reflect before taking action.

# 2
# ENERGY LEVELS

# 2

## Energy Levels

In magic, energy level refers to the amount of life force and mental focus a practitioner is able to gather when performing a spell.

The effectiveness of the ritual will largely depend on how much energy can be directed toward its purpose.

## There are three main energy levels when practicing magic:

**1. Low Energy (Weak or Ineffective Spell)**

-Feeling of fatigue, apathy, or lack of concentration.

-Presence of doubt, fear, or insecurity about the ritual.

-Lack of emotion or weak connection with the magical intention.

-Physical or mental exhaustion.

**2. Medium Energy (Spell with Moderate Results)**

-Focused mind, though with slight distractions.

-Stable energy level but without high intensity.

-Connection with the spell's purpose, though not at full potential.

**3. High Energy (Highly Effective Spell)**

-Complete confidence in the success of the ritual.

-Deep state of concentration, where mind and body are in sync.

-Intense emotion aligned with the magical purpose.

-Clear and detailed visualization of the desired outcome.

## How to Raise Your Energy Level Before a Ritual

To increase personal energy before performing magic, it is essential to prepare the body, mind, and spirit.

### 1. Care for the Body and Mind

-Proper rest: Sleeping well before a ritual helps prevent fatigue and improves concentration.

-Physical exercise: Keeps energy flowing and strengthens the connection with the body.

-Healthy diet: Prioritize natural foods and avoid excessive sugar or heavy meals before practicing magic.

-Hydration: Drinking water or herbal infusions supports a better flow of energy throughout the body.

### 2. Techniques to Raise Personal Energy

-Purification bath: Use sea salt, rosemary, and lavender before casting a spell to cleanse your energy.

-Deep breathing: Slowly inhale and exhale in a controlled manner to oxygenate the body and improve focus.

-Activating movements: Shake your hands, stretch, or move your arms in circles to awaken inner energy.

-Natural energy charging: Expose yourself to sunlight to absorb vitality or to moonlight to work on intuition and emotional balance.

## 3. The Importance of Mental State in Magic

The mind plays a key role in the effectiveness of a spell, as it acts as a channel that directs energy toward the desired intention.

If a ritual is performed with doubt or negative emotions, the energy will become scattered and its effectiveness will be reduced.

Factors that influence mental state during a spell:

-Self-confidence: Strong belief in the effectiveness of the ritual.

-Emotion aligned with the purpose: Internally feeling the emotion of the manifested desire.

-Total concentration: Keeping the mind focused solely on the magical intention.

-Distraction-free environment: Turn off electronic devices and work in a calm and harmonious space.

## 4. Strategies to Achieve an Ideal Mental State Before the Ritual

### 4.1 Meditation and Mental Control

-Pre-ritual meditation: Calms the mind and strengthens the connection with the magical intention.

-Guided visualization: Clearly imagine the result of the spell before performing it.

-Mantras and affirmations: Repeat empowering phrases to reinforce confidence in your magical practice.

## 4.2 Using Sound to Raise Vibration

-Energy frequencies: Listening to sounds at 528 Hz or 432 Hz supports spiritual activation.

-Shamanic or instrumental music: Elevates energy and enhances concentration.

## 4.3 Energetic Breathing Techniques

-Breath of fire: Quick inhalations and exhalations to activate life force energy.

-Conscious breathing: Inhale for 4 counts, hold for 4 counts, and exhale for 4 counts.

## 4.4 Mental Reprogramming with Positive Affirmations

Affirmations help strengthen the mind and raise energy before a ritual.

### Examples of affirmations before a spell:

-"My energy is strong and my magic is powerful."

-"I trust in my ability to manifest my desires."

-"Every spell I cast is successful."

-"I am a channel of pure energy and my intentions flow with ease."

-"The universe supports my magical purposes."

### How to use them:

-Repeat them out loud or mentally before the ritual.

-Write them down and read them before lighting a candle.

-Record them on a device and listen to them before sleeping.

## 4.5 How to Maintain a High Energy Level During a Ritual

To ensure the spell is performed with maximum energy, it's helpful to apply these methods:

-Rub your palms together or tap them lightly before channeling energy.

-Visualize a bright light coming from your chest or hands toward the purpose of the ritual.

-Feel and act as if the desire has already been fulfilled.

## 4.6 Signs That Energy in a Spell Is Low

If you experience any of the following symptoms during the ritual, it's likely that the energy isn't flowing properly:

-Lack of emotion or enthusiasm during the spell.

-Sudden feeling of exhaustion or fatigue.

-Scattered thoughts or constant doubts.

-Disconnection from the ritual's intention.

## How to Fix This?

If you notice these signs, stop the ritual and do energy-raising exercises again before trying once more.

# 3

# HOW TO WORK WITH THE MOON'S ENERGY

# 3

## How to Work with the Moon's Energy

Since ancient times, the moon has been a source of power for magic and spirituality.

Its influence extends not only to nature but also to our emotions and the effectiveness of rituals.

Each lunar phase carries a unique vibration that can enhance different types of spells and magical practices.

Understanding its influence allows you to align your own energy with the natural cycles of the universe and harness its power at the right time.

### Why is the Moon Important in Magic?

-Its influence over tides and emotions affects our subconscious and the way we manifest our intentions.

-Each lunar phase emits a different energetic frequency, which determines whether a spell will be more effective or if it's better to wait.

-Working in harmony with the moon allows you to connect with natural rhythms and amplify your personal power.

### 1. New Moon: Beginnings and Renewal

The New Moon marks the beginning of a new cycle, symbolizing a chance for renewal and the planting of intentions. It is a phase of introspection and limitless potential, ideal for setting goals, planning for the future, and working on personal growth.

**Uses in Magic:**

-Starting projects or establishing new habits

-Enhancing spiritual connection and intuition

-Performing cleansing rituals and preparing for new paths

-Setting intentions that will expand in the following lunar phases

Tip: During this phase, attraction spells work best when focused on the initial intention, allowing the energy to grow with the lunar cycle.

## 2. Waxing Moon: Expansion and Progress

As the moon grows brighter, its energy becomes ideal for growth and for strengthening what was initiated during the New Moon. It is a phase of momentum and determination, perfect for attracting what we want in our lives.

**Uses in Magic:**

-Spells to attract love, prosperity, and opportunities
-Rituals to boost confidence, vitality, and motivation
-Magical work aimed at achieving success in personal or professional projects
-Development of self-love and personal evolution

Tip: During this time, the energy of rituals builds quickly, making it a great moment to reinforce intentions and take action in everyday life.

## 3. Full Moon: Power and Manifestation

When the moon is fully illuminated, its energy reaches its peak, amplifying magic and spiritual connection.

This phase is the most intense and powerful of the lunar cycle, making it ideal for enhancing any type of spell.

**Uses in Magic:**

-Manifestation rituals to bring desires and projects into reality
-Spells for love, abundance, success, and protection
-Activation of intuition and development of psychic abilities
-Energetic recharging of crystals, magical tools, and amulets

Tip: Since the Full Moon intensifies emotions, it's important to channel the energy properly to avoid exhaustion or scattering. Keeping a clear intention will ensure effective magical work.

## 4. Waning Moon: Release and Purification

After the brilliance of the Full Moon, the waning phase begins —a period of introspection and cleansing. This is the ideal time to let go of what no longer serves us and to remove negative energies or blockages.

**Uses in Magic:**

-Personal or home cleansing and purification rituals
-Spells to cut toxic ties and eliminate limiting patterns
-Protection against negative energies and strengthening of the aura
-Emotional detox and inner healing

Tip: The Waning Moon supports release and renewal, making it ideal for closing cycles and preparing for the next New Moon.

# 4

# LOVE, RELATIONSHIPS, AND FERTILITY

# 4.1

**Self-Love Spell**

## 1. Purpose:

This spell is designed to enhance self-love,
strengthen self-esteem, and balance inner energy.
It is based on connecting with your personal essence,
practicing self-care, and encouraging self-healing.

This ritual will help you:

-Boost your self-esteem
-Attract positive energies
-Heal emotional wounds
-Increase self-confidence
-Deepen self-love and acceptance

## 2. Optimal Lunar Phase:

Waxing Moon or Full Moon: Ideal for enhancing growth,
fulfillment, and self-empowerment.

## 3. Materials:

-1 pink candle (for self-love and self-esteem)
-1 white candle (for healing and purification)
-Rose petals (for love and harmony)
-Chamomile (for calm and emotional well-being)
-Rosemary (for protection and inner strength)
-Lavender oil (for relaxation and self-love)
-Jasmine oil (for confidence and inner beauty)
-Rose quartz (for self-love and healing)
-Amethyst (for emotional balance and inner peace)
-Tarot card: The Empress (beauty, love, and self-affirmation)

-Tarot card: The Sun (fulfillment and personal happiness)
-Tarot card: The Star (hope and self-acceptance)

## 4. Procedure:

1. Find a quiet place free from distractions.
Light sandalwood or palo santo incense to cleanse the
energy.

2. Anoint the candles with lavender and jasmine oils, from the
base to the wick. Sprinkle the rose petals and herbs around
them. Place the rose quartz and amethyst next to the candles.

3. In the center, place The Empress. To the left, The Sun
(to radiate love and happiness). To the right, The Star (to
remind you of your worth and inner light).

4. Light the white candle first, saying: "I purify my energy,
I release fears and doubts. I am at peace with myself."
Then, light the pink candle, saying: "I love and accept
myself just as I am. My light shines with strength and love."

5. With your hands over the tarot cards and your eyes on
the candle flames, repeat with conviction: "I am light, I am
love, I am strength and harmony. In every heartbeat, my
divine essence vibrates. I love, value, and respect myself.
My energy shines with purity and confidence. I am enough,
I am worthy, I am whole. So it is, so shall it be."

6. Close your eyes and breathe deeply. Imagine a pink light
surrounding you, filling you with love and confidence. Feel
the energy of self-love growing within you.

## 5. Closing the Ritual:

1. Give thanks to the universe and to yourself for this moment
of connection.

2. Let the candles burn out (or extinguish them with your

fingers if you need to pause the ritual and repeat it over several nights).

3. Keep the rose quartz with you or place it on your nightstand.

## 6. Duration:

The effects begin to be felt in the following days, as you strengthen your self-love. You can repeat the spell each month during the waxing moon to enhance it.

## 7. Extra tip:

Write a self-love affirmation on a piece of paper and read it every morning to keep the energy of the ritual alive.

# 4.2

## Fertility Spell for Couples

VI
THE LOVERS

### 1. Purpose:

This spell is designed to enhance fertility in couples, balance the body's energy, and open pathways to conception. It focuses on the loving connection between partners and harmonizing the physical and spiritual body to welcome new life.

This ritual will help you:

-Increase fertility in the couple.
-Balance feminine and masculine energies.
-Heal emotional or energetic blockages that may hinder conception.
-Attract blessings of abundance and fertility.

### 2. Optimal Moon Phase:

Waxing Moon or Full Moon: To enhance expansion and the creation of life.

### 3. Materials:

-1 green candle (fertility, growth, and health)
-1 white candle (purity and blessings)
-1 pink candle (love and connection in the couple)
-Basil (fertility and harmony)
-Chamomile (calm and receptivity)
-Cinnamon (warmth and energy for conception)
-Rose oil (love and feminine energy)
-Sandalwood oil (masculine energy and balance)
-Rose quartz (love and connection)
-Moonstone (fertility and feminine energy)

-Tarot card: The Empress (fertility and abundance)
-Tarot card: The Sun (vitality and life energy)
-Tarot card: Two of Cups (love and connection in the couple)

## 4. Procedure:

1. Find a quiet place where you can perform the ritual with your partner or alone if you prefer. Cleanse the space with lavender or sandalwood incense to attract harmonious energies.

2. Anoint the candles with rose and sandalwood oils, from the base to the wick. Sprinkle the herbs around the candles in a circle. Place the rose quartz and moonstone next to the candles.

3. In the center, place The Empress (representing fertility). To her left, place The Sun (to bring strength and vitality). To her right, place The Two of Cups (to strengthen the loving bond and connection as a couple).

4. First, light the white candle, saying: "May the purity and blessing of life surround us." Then, light the green candle, saying: "May fertility and abundance flow through our bodies." Finally, light the pink candle, saying: "May love and connection unite us in this creation."

5. With your hands over the tarot cards and your eyes on the candle flames, repeat with conviction: "Mother Earth, sacred force, nourish our bodies, bless our love, may the seed of life sprout with light and love, may the miracle of fertility manifest. So it is, so it shall be."

6. Close your eyes and take deep breaths. Imagine a golden light surrounding you and your partner, filling your bodies with fertile energy. If you're with your partner, hold hands and feel the connection.

## 5. Closing the Ritual:

1. Give thanks to the universe and the energy of life.

2. Let the candles burn out or extinguish them with your fingers if you wish to repeat the ritual over several nights.

3. Place the moonstone under your pillow to reinforce its energy.

## 6. Duration:

The effects may be felt during the following lunar cycles. Repeat the ritual during each waxing moon until conception manifests.

## 7. Extra Tip:

In the following days, reinforce the spell with daily affirmations such as: "My body is fertile and receptive," and carry the rose quartz with you to keep the energy of love and fertility active.

# 4.3

## Spell to Attract Your Soulmate

THE LOVERS

### 1. Purpose:

This spell is designed to attract your soulmate—the person with whom you share a deep spiritual connection. It doesn't seek to force love but to align your energy with the vibration of true love and allow the universe to guide that person to you.

This ritual will help you:

-Attract your soulmate
-Open paths to true love
-Remove emotional blockages that prevent connection
-Enhance the energy of love and harmony

### 2. Optimal Moon Phase:

Waxing Moon or Full Moon: To strengthen attraction and the manifestation of love.

### 3. Materials:

-1 red candle (for passion and loving energy)
-1 pink candle (for pure love and harmony)
-1 white candle (for spiritual connection and clarity)
-Rose petals (love and romance)
-Ground cinnamon (attraction and warmth)
-Lavender (emotional balance and spiritual connection)
-Rose essential oil (unconditional love)
-Jasmine oil (seduction and attraction)
-Rose quartz (love and connection)
-Amethyst (harmonization and spiritual elevation)
-Clear quartz (clarity in the connection)

-Tarot card: The Lovers (true love and soul connection)
-Tarot card: The Star (destiny and hope in love)
-Tarot card: Two of Cups (soul union and mutual love)

## 4. Procedure:

1. Find a quiet place without interruptions. Cleanse the area with sandalwood or palo santo incense to purify the energy.

2. Anoint the candles with rose and jasmine oils, from the base to the wick, while visualizing the love you wish to attract. Sprinkle a bit of cinnamon and rose petals around the candles. Place the rose quartz, amethyst, and clear quartz next to the candles.

3. Place The Lovers card in the center. On the left, place The Star to guide destiny. On the right, place The Two of Cups for loving union.

4. First, light the white candle, saying: "May clarity and light guide my soul to true connection." Then light the pink candle, saying: "May love and harmony fill my life and heart." Finally, light the red candle, saying: "May the passion and energy of true love manifest in my life."

5. With your hands over the tarot cards and your eyes on the candle flames, repeat with conviction: "Universe, destiny, and eternal love, guide me to my soulmate, may our hearts recognize each other, may our paths cross, and may love bloom with truth and harmony. So it is, so it shall be."

6. Close your eyes and breathe deeply. Imagine a pink light surrounding you, filling you with love and confidence. Visualize that light traveling through the universe until it connects with the energy of your soulmate.

## 5. Closing the Ritual:

1. Thank the universe for the energy received.

2. Let the candles burn out (or extinguish them with your fingers if you need to pause the ritual and repeat it over several nights).

3. Keep the rose quartz with you or place it on your nightstand.

## 6. Duration:

The spell begins to take effect in the following weeks or months, depending on your openness and alignment with the universe. You can repeat it for three consecutive nights during the waxing or full moon.

## 7. Extra Tip:

If after the ritual you notice signs like repeated numbers (11:11), dreams about someone special, or unexpected encounters, it may be a sign that your soulmate is near.

# 4.4

## Emotional Healing and Past Release Spell

THE LOVERS

## 1. Purpose:

This spell is designed to heal emotional wounds, cut ties with past experiences that are holding you back, and help you find inner peace. It is based on the energy of renewal and personal transformation.

This ritual will help you:

-Heal emotional wounds from the past
-Release emotional and energetic blockages
-Cut ties with people or situations that hinder personal growth
-Attract peace, balance, and emotional clarity

## 2. Optimal Moon Phase:

Waning Moon: Ideal for releasing, cleansing, and letting go of what no longer serves you.

## 3. Materials:

-1 white candle (healing and purification)
-1 blue candle (peace and emotional clarity)
-1 purple candle (transformation and spiritual elevation)
-Sage (cleansing and purification)
-Lavender (calm and emotional well-being)
-Rue (protection and removal of negative energies)
-Lavender oil (relaxation and healing)
-Eucalyptus oil (cleansing and release)
-Amethyst (transmutation of negative energies)
-Rose quartz (self-love and emotional healing)
-Black obsidian (protection and cutting toxic ties)

-Tarot card: Death (renewal and transformation)
-Tarot card: Judgment (release and closure of cycles)
-Tarot card: The Star (hope and healing)

## 4. Procedure:

1. Find a quiet place where you can be at peace.
Cleanse the area with sage or palo santo incense
to remove stagnant energies.

2. Anoint the candles with lavender and eucalyptus oils,
from the base to the wick. Sprinkle a bit of lavender and
rue around the candles. Place the amethyst, rose quartz,
and obsidian near the candles.

3. In the center, place Death (symbolizing the end of what
must be released). To the left, place Judgment (to free
yourself from the weight of the past). To the right, place
The Star (to attract healing and renewal).

4. Light the white candle first, saying: "Healing light, purify
my soul and heart." Then light the blue candle, saying:
"May peace and serenity fill my being." Finally, light the purple
candle, saying: "I transform my pain into wisdom and growth."

5. With your hands over the tarot cards and your eyes on
the candle flames, repeat with conviction: "Today I release
the past and heal my soul, everything that hurt me dissolves
into light, I allow myself to let go, I allow myself to heal, my
heart opens to peace and happiness. So it is, so it shall be."

6. Close your eyes and take a deep breath. Imagine a violet
light surrounding you, dissolving all emotional weight from
the past. Visualize yourself shedding the energy of painful
experiences and being filled with peace.

## 5. Closing the Ritual:

1. Thank the universe for the healing received.

2. If you wish, write down everything you want to release on a piece of paper and burn it in the flame of the purple candle.

3. Let the candles burn out (or extinguish them with your fingers if you need to repeat the ritual over several nights).

5. Keep the amethyst with you to continue working on the transmutation of energies.

## 6. Duration:

The effects begin to be felt in the following days, bringing peace and emotional clarity. You can repeat the ritual during each waning moon until you feel fully liberated.

## 7. Extra Tip:

In the following days, write release affirmations such as:

-I let go of the past and open myself to new opportunities for happiness.

-I release everything that no longer serves me and welcome the new with love and gratitude.

-I free myself from the burdens of the past and walk lightly toward my destiny.

-I trust the process of life and know that everything happens for my highest good.

-Today I release fear and allow peace to guide my path.

-"I forgive, I release, and I allow myself to move forward with confidence and joy."

# 4.5

### Sexual Passion Spell

THE LOVERS

## 1. Purpose:

This spell is designed to ignite passion in a relationship, increase attraction, and strengthen the sexual connection between two people. It can also be used to awaken your own sensual energy and attract passionate experiences.

This ritual will help you:

-Increase passion and sexual desire in a relationship
-Enhance personal attraction and magnetism
-Awaken sensuality and self-confidence
-Rekindle the spark in romantic relationships

## 2. Optimal Moon Phase:

Waxing Moon or Full Moon: To enhance energy and attraction.

## 3. Materials:

-1 red candle (for desire and passion)
-1 black candle (for attraction and sexual magnetism)
-1 pink candle (to maintain love and tenderness along with passion)
-Cinnamon (boosts attraction and desire)
-Ginger (increases sexual energy)
-Red rose petals (love and sensuality)
-Jasmine oil (awakens sensuality)
-Musk oil (intensifies attraction)
-Garnet (passion and sexual energy)
-Red quartz (boosts desire and vitality)
-Black obsidian (releases sexual and energetic blockages)

-Tarot card: The Devil (intense passion and physical desire)
-Tarot card: The Lovers (romantic and sexual connection)
-Tarot card: Ace of Wands (overflowing sexual energy)

## 4. Procedure:

1. Choose a place where you feel comfortable. You can play sensual music and light vanilla or sandalwood incense to enhance the energy.

2. Anoint the candles with jasmine and musk oils, from the base to the wick, visualizing passion growing in your life. Sprinkle cinnamon and rose petals around the candles. Place the garnet, red quartz, and obsidian near the candles.

3. In the center, place The Devil (to ignite passion and desire). To the left, place The Lovers (to strengthen the romantic connection). To the right, place Ace of Wands (to stimulate sexual energy).

4. Light the black candle first, saying: "May desire awaken and attraction grow." Then light the red candle, saying: "May passion burn with intensity and pleasure." Finally, light the pink candle, saying: "May love and tenderness be the foundation of this union."

5. With your hands over the tarot cards and your eyes on the candle flames, repeat with conviction: "Fire of passion, awaken within me, may attraction intensify and desire be reborn. May love and pleasure merge in harmony, and may the spark never fade. So it is, so it shall be."

6. Close your eyes and feel the burning energy of desire within you. Visualize passion and attraction flowing into your life, growing stronger with each breath. If the spell is for a partner, imagine the connection between you both deepening.

## 5. Closing the Ritual:

1. Thank the universe and the energy of fire for the passion awakened.

2. Let the candles burn out (or extinguish them with your fingers if you need to repeat the ritual over several nights).

3. Keep the garnet with you to maintain the energy of passion.

## 6. Duration:

The effect may begin to be felt in the following days, intensifying desire and attraction. You can repeat the ritual during each waxing moon to keep the passion alive.

## 7. Extra Tip:

Wear red clothing or a musk perfume in the days that follow to keep the energy of the spell active.

# 4.6

## Long-Lasting Love Spell

### 1. Purpose:

This spell is designed to strengthen love in a relationship and ensure it is long-lasting, built on trust, passion, respect, and harmony. It focuses on solidifying the bond and keeping away energies that could weaken the connection over time.

This ritual will help you:

-Strengthen and prolong love in a relationship
-Create a solid foundation of trust and stability
-Rekindle the spark and passion over time
-Protect the relationship from negative external influences

### 2. Optimal Moon Phase:

Waxing Moon or Full Moon: To enhance stability, growth, and fulfillment in love.

### 3. Materials:

-2 red candles (passion and lasting love)
-1 white candle (harmony and peace in the relationship)
-1 gold candle (commitment and stability)
-Red rose petals (love and romance)
-Cinnamon (warmth and permanence in the relationship)
-Rosemary (protection and fidelity)
-Jasmine oil (attraction and love)
-Musk oil (connection and mutual desire)
-Rose quartz (unconditional love and union)
-Red agate (stability and loyalty)
-Amethyst (protection and emotional balance)

-Tarot card: The Lovers (true love and deep connection)
-Tarot card: The Hierophant (commitment and stability)
-Tarot card: Ten of Cups (emotional fulfillment and happiness in a relationship)

## 4. Procedure:

1. Find a quiet place without interruptions. Light rose or sandalwood incense to harmonize the energy.

2. Anoint the candles with jasmine and musk oils, from the base to the wick, visualizing a strong and lasting romantic relationship. Sprinkle cinnamon and rose petals around the candles. Place the rose quartz, red agate, and amethyst near the candles.

3. In the center, place The Lovers (representing love and connection in the couple). To the left, place The Hierophant (for stability and commitment). To the right, place Ten of Cups (for fulfillment and happiness in the relationship).

4. First, light the white candle, saying: "May peace and harmony reign in our relationship." Then light the two red candles, saying: "May passion and love unite us more each day." Finally, light the gold candle, saying: "May stability and loyalty strengthen our bond."

5. With your hands over the tarot cards and your eyes on the candle flames, repeat with conviction: "The love that binds us is eternal and strong, it grows with the years and is blessed all along. May our passion never fade, may trust protect us and love never be swayed. So it is, so it shall be."

6. Close your eyes and take a deep breath. Visualize yourself and your partner together, happy, and growing in love over the years. Feel the energy of commitment and fulfillment surrounding you both.

## 5. Closing the Ritual:

1. Thank the universe for the blessing of love.

2. If you wish, write both of your names on a piece of paper along with the phrase "eternal love" and keep it in a special place.

3. Let the candles burn out (or extinguish them with your fingers if you need to repeat the ritual over several nights).

4. Keep the rose quartz with you or place it in the couple's room.

## 6. Duration:

The effects begin to be felt in the following weeks, strengthening emotional connection and stability in the relationship. You can repeat the ritual during each full moon to maintain the energy of lasting love.

## 7. Extra Tip:

To reinforce the energy of the spell, exchange with your partner an object charged with your love (this could be an amulet, a letter, or an item of clothing).

# 4.7

## Spell to Break a Toxic Relationship

VI
THE LOVERS

### 1. Purpose:

This spell is designed to sever ties with a relationship that causes emotional harm, dependency, or energetic blockages. Its purpose is to free the person from negative attachments and open the path to healing and personal growth.

This ritual will help you:

-Cut emotional ties with a toxic relationship
-Break patterns of dependency and suffering
-Protect yourself from manipulation and negative energies
-Strengthen self-trust and self-love to move forward

### 2. Optimal Moon Phase:

Waning Moon: Ideal for eliminating, releasing, and breaking harmful ties.

### 3. Materials:

-1 black candle (to absorb negativity and close cycles)
-1 white candle (for protection and healing)
-1 red candle (to restore personal energy and strength)
-Rue (to drive away negative energies and cut ties)
-Sage (to purify the soul and mind)
-Rosemary (for protection and clarity)
-Eucalyptus oil (to release and clear the mind)
-Lavender oil (to heal the heart)
-Black obsidian (protection and cutting toxic bonds)
-Amethyst (transmutation and emotional balance)

-Rose quartz (emotional healing and self-love)
-Tarot card: The Tower (breakup, drastic transformation)
-Tarot card: The Devil (emotional dependencies and toxic relationships)
-Tarot card: The Fool (freedom and new beginnings)

## 4. Procedure:

1. Find a quiet place where you can perform the ritual without interruptions. Purify the space with sage or palo santo incense.

2. Anoint the black candle with eucalyptus oil, visualizing it absorbing all the negative energy from the relationship. Anoint the white candle with lavender oil, visualizing your heart healing. Anoint the red candle with the same oil, asking for strength and determination. Sprinkle rue and rosemary around the candles. Place the black obsidian, amethyst, and rose quartz near the candles.

3. In the center, place The Tower (symbolizing the breakup of the relationship). To the left, place The Devil (representing the toxicity being released). To the right, place The Fool (symbolizing new beginnings and freedom).

4. Light the black candle first, saying: "I cut the ties that bind me to this toxic relationship." Then light the white candle, saying: "I release myself in peace and protection, I heal my soul and my heart." Finally, light the red candle, saying: "I reclaim my strength and energy, I move forward with determination and confidence."

5. With your hands over the tarot cards and your eyes on the candle flames, repeat with conviction: "Today I break the chains that bind me, my soul is free, my heart is healed. Light and truth guide me, the past dissolves and the future awaits. So it is, so it shall be."

6. Close your eyes and visualize the ties between you and

the toxic person breaking. Imagine a white light surrounding and protecting you. Feel the relief and peace of being free from that relationship.

## 5. Closing the Ritual:

1. Thank the universe for the release.

2. Write the name of the person or the feelings you wish to let go of on a piece of paper and burn it in the flame of the black candle.

3. Let the candles burn out (or extinguish them with your fingers if you need to repeat the ritual over several nights).

4. Keep the black obsidian with you to continue protecting yourself.

## 6. Duration:

The effects begin to be felt in the following days, bringing emotional clarity and inner peace. You can repeat the ritual during each waning moon until you feel completely free.

## 7. Extra Tip:

Block contact with the toxic person on social media and avoid places or habits that connect you to that relationship.

# 4.8

**Spell to Remove Blockages and
Limitations in Love**

THE LOVERS

## 1. Purpose:

This spell is designed to eliminate emotional blockages,
insecurities, or traumas that prevent love from flowing
freely in your life. It can be used to attract a healthy
romantic relationship or to heal an existing one that
is facing obstacles.

This ritual will help you:

-Remove emotional blockages that prevent love from
entering your life
-Heal past wounds that create fear or distrust
-Open your heart to new romantic opportunities
-Release negative patterns in relationships

## 2. Optimal Moon Phase:

-Waning Moon: To eliminate blockages and barriers
-Waxing Moon: To open paths and allow love to enter

## 3. Materials:

-1 white candle (for purification and healing)
-1 pink candle (for self-love and romantic love)
-1 blue candle (for clarity and loving communication)
-Lavender (to soothe the heart and release the past)
-Rue (to remove negative energies and blockages)
-Rose petals (to attract pure love and harmony)
-Jasmine oil (to open the heart to love)
-Eucalyptus oil (to clear emotional blockages)
-Amethyst (to transmute negative energies and heal the past)

-Rose quartz (to attract love and heal the heart)
-Black obsidian (to break toxic patterns in love)
-Tarot card: The Moon (fears, illusions, and unconscious blockages)
-Tarot card: Judgment (release and rebirth)
-Tarot card: Two of Cups (healthy and balanced love)

## 4. Procedure:

1. Find a quiet place where you won't be disturbed.
Light lavender or sandalwood incense to purify the space.

2. Anoint the candles with jasmine and eucalyptus oils, from the base to the wick, visualizing negative energy dissolving and love flowing freely into your life. Sprinkle rue and rose petals around the candles. Place the amethyst, rose quartz, and black obsidian near the candles.

3. In the center, place The Moon (representing emotional blockages and fear in love). To the left, place Judgment (for the release of those blockages). To the right, place Two of Cups (symbolizing the arrival of sincere and balanced love).

4. Light the white candle first, saying: "I purify my heart and soul of all fear and doubt." Then light the blue candle, saying: "I release the chains of the past and open my heart." Finally, light the pink candle, saying: "Love flows into my life with harmony and fullness."

5. With your hands over the tarot cards and your eyes on the candle flames, repeat with conviction: "I break the barriers, I release the pain, my heart is free and ready for love again. The light of truth guides my way, and true love is coming to stay. So it is, so it shall be."

6. Close your eyes and take a deep breath. Imagine a golden light surrounding your heart, dissolving any blockages. Visualize love flowing freely into your life, without fear or limitations.

## 5. Closing the Ritual:

1. Thank the universe for the healing and release received.
2. Write down the fears or blockages you wish to let go of on a piece of paper and burn it in the flame of the white candle.
3. Let the candles burn out (or extinguish them with your fingers if you wish to repeat the ritual over several nights).
4. Keep the rose quartz with you to maintain the energy of love in your life.

## 6. Duration:

The effect begins to be felt in the following weeks, bringing emotional clarity and healthier romantic opportunities.
You can repeat the ritual during each waning or waxing moon as needed.

## 7. Extra Tip:

Every morning, repeat affirmations such as:

-I am open to sincere and healthy love. I deserve a fulfilling and harmonious relationship.
-I open my heart to love and allow it to flow freely into my life.
-I deserve a love that is sincere, healthy, and full of harmony.
-I release the wounds of the past and allow myself to love and be loved fully.
-I am worthy of a true love that nurtures my soul and my heart.
-I break free from all limiting beliefs about love and make space for new opportunities.
-I attract a partner into my life who values me, respects me, and loves me authentically.

# 5
# MONEY AND PROSPERITY

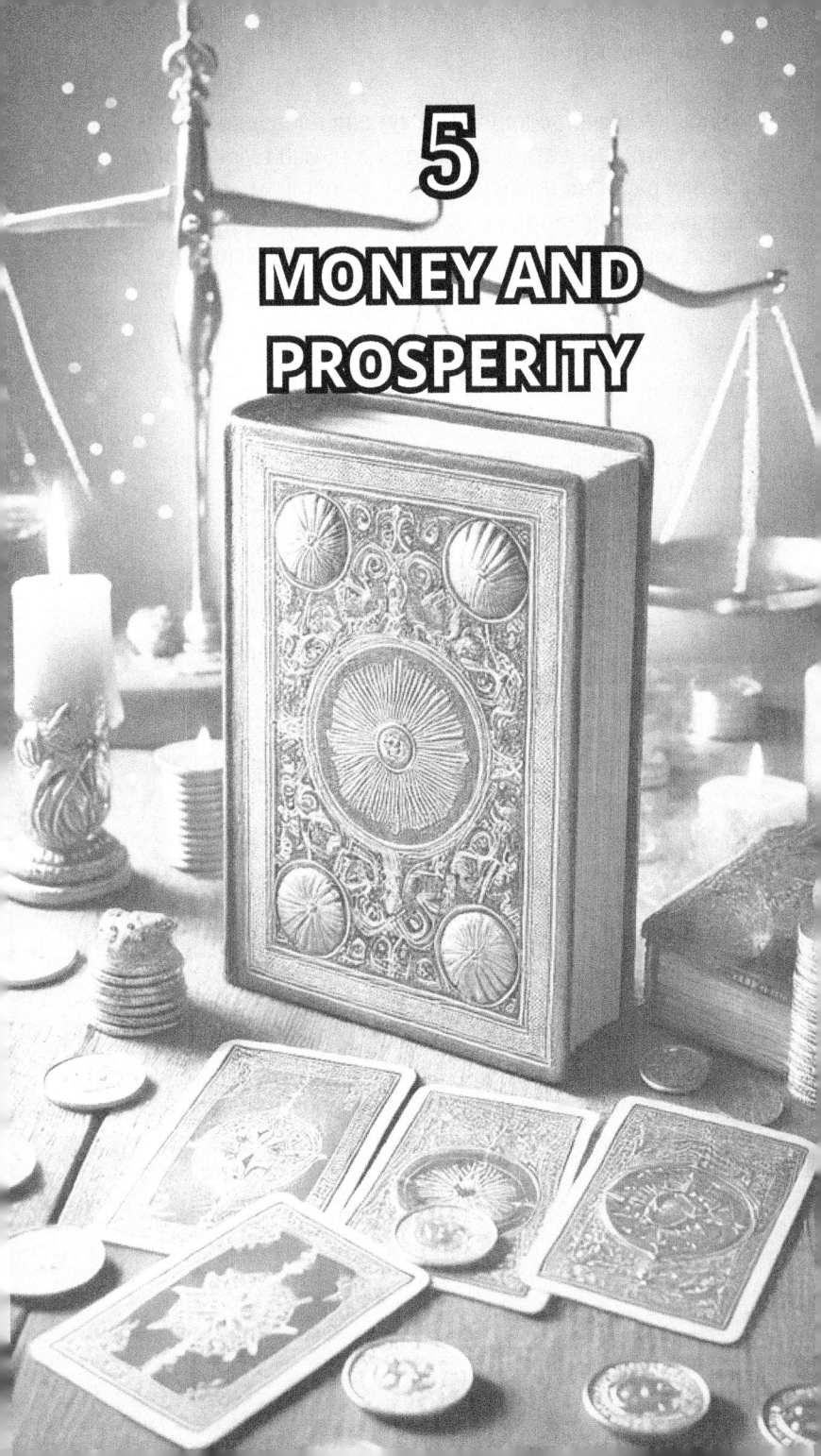

# 5.1

### Spell for Wealth and Abundance

KING of PENTACLES

## 1. Purpose:

This spell is designed to attract economic prosperity, financial opportunities, and material stability. It helps remove blockages that prevent the flow of money and aligns your energy with abundance.

This ritual will help you:

-Attract wealth and financial stability.
-Open paths to new financial opportunities.
-Eliminate blockages that hinder prosperity.
-Increase confidence in your ability to generate abundance.

## 2. Optimal Moon Phase:

Waxing Moon or Full Moon: To enhance financial growth and expansion.

## 3. Materials:

-1 gold candle (represents wealth and success)
-1 green candle (for prosperity and abundance)
-1 white candle (for clarity and energetic cleansing)
-Cinnamon (attracts money and luck)
-Bay leaf (symbol of success and financial triumph)
-Basil (energy of abundance and economic protection)
-Sandalwood oil (to attract success and prosperity)
-Orange oil (for motivation and business optimism)
-Pyrite (magnet for wealth and financial opportunities)
-Citrine (energy of success and money attraction)
-Green jade (lasting prosperity and economic growth).

-Tarot card: The Emperor (financial stability and authority in business).
-Tarot card: The Nine of Pentacles (material abundance and satisfaction).
-Tarot card: The Ace of Pentacles (new economic opportunities and prosperity).

**4. Procedure:**

1. Find a quiet place free from interruptions. Light sandalwood or cinnamon incense to cleanse the energy of the space.

2. Anoint the candles with sandalwood and orange oils, from the base to the wick, while visualizing money and opportunities flowing into your life. Sprinkle cinnamon and bay leaves around the candles. Place the pyrite, citrine, and green jade near the candles.

3. In the center, place "The Emperor" (represents financial stability and control over wealth). To the left, place "The Nine of Pentacles" (symbolizes abundance and financial independence). To the right, place "The Ace of Pentacles" (attracts new financial opportunities).

4. First, light the white candle, saying: "I purify my energy and remove all barriers to abundance." Then light the gold candle, saying: "Wealth flows into my life with ease and gratitude." Finally, light the green candle, saying: "Prosperity and success are mine, today and always."

5. With your hands over the tarot cards and your eyes on the candle flames, repeat with conviction: "Gold and fortune come to me, abundance grows and never ends. Success and wealth fill my being, the universe blesses me with its power. So it is, so it shall be."

6. Close your eyes and take a deep breath. Imagine a golden stream of energy flowing toward you, filling you with wealth and opportunities. Visualize money entering your life

consistently and securely.

## 5. Closing the ritual:

1. Thank the universe for the prosperity received.

2. Write a positive affirmation on a piece of paper, such as: "I am a magnet for wealth and success," and keep it in your wallet.

3. Let the candles burn out (or extinguish them with your fingers if you plan to repeat the ritual over several nights).

4. Carry the citrine or pyrite with you to keep the energy of abundance active.

## 6. Duration:

The effects may be felt in the following weeks with new financial opportunities and greater stability. You can repeat the ritual during each waxing moon or full moon to strengthen its power.

## 7. Extra tip:

Write down the amount of money you wish to receive and place it under the pyrite until it manifests.

# 5.2

## Spell for Work and Employment

KING OF PENTACLES

### 1. Purpose:

This spell is designed to attract a new job, improve job stability, or open paths to successful professional opportunities. It focuses on unblocking stagnant energy and attracting recognition and success in the workplace.

This ritual will help you:

-Get a new job or improve your current one.
-Attract professional opportunities and recognition.
-Remove blockages that hinder career growth.
-Enhance confidence and security in interviews and projects.

### 2. Optimal Moon Phase:

Waxing Moon or Full Moon: To attract new opportunities and professional success.

### 3. Materials:

-1 gold candle (for success and recognition)
-1 green candle (for job prosperity)
-1 blue candle (for clarity and communication in interviews or business)
-Bay leaves (symbol of success and triumph at work)
-Rosemary (for protection and professional growth)
-Cinnamon (to attract opportunities and prosperity)
-Sandalwood oil (to boost work-related energy)
-Lemon oil (for mental clarity and decision-making)
-Citrine (attracts professional success and opportunities)
-Pyrite (magnet for wealth and recognition)

-Tiger's Eye (protection and confidence in the workplace)
-Tarot card: The Magician (skills and new job opportunities)
-Tarot card: The Ace of Pentacles (new job offers and financial stability)
-Tarot card: The Six of Wands (success, recognition, and achievements)

## 4. Procedure:

1. Find a quiet place free from interruptions. Light sandalwood or lemon incense to cleanse the energy and attract success.

2. Anoint the candles with sandalwood and lemon oils, from the base to the wick, visualizing success and job stability. Sprinkle bay leaves, cinnamon, and rosemary around the candles. Place the citrine, pyrite, and tiger's eye near the candles.

3. In the center, place "The Magician" (symbolizing creativity and the ability to attract opportunities). To the left, place "The Ace of Pentacles" (for the arrival of new job offers). To the right, place "The Six of Wands" (for recognition and professional success).

4. First, light the gold candle, saying: "Success and abundance are entering my life." Then light the green candle, saying: "I open the path to a prosperous and stable job." Finally, light the blue candle, saying: "Clarity and confidence guide me on my professional path."

5. With your hands over the tarot cards and your eyes on the candle flames, repeat with conviction: "Universe of opportunities, hear me well, bring to me the job I deserve to have. May success find me and stability follow, may the doors of employment open with joy. So it is, so it shall be."

6. Close your eyes and take a deep breath. Imagine a golden door opening in front of you and stepping into a place where you work happily and successfully. Visualize a job offer

coming to you or being recognized in your current job.

## 5. Closing the ritual:

1. Thank the universe for the opportunities received.

2. Write the phrase on a piece of paper: "I am ready
to receive a prosperous and stable job," and keep it
in your wallet or on your desk.

3. Let the candles burn out (or extinguish them with your
fingers if you wish to repeat the ritual over several nights).

4. Carry the citrine or pyrite with you to maintain the energy
of success and opportunity.

## 6. Duration:

The effects may be felt in the following weeks through
new job opportunities or improvements in your current job.
You can repeat the ritual during each waxing moon or full
moon
to enhance its power.

## 7. Extra tip:

Carry a bay leaf in your wallet or briefcase and write on it:
"Success and job stability," to keep the spell's energy active.

# 5.3

## Spell for Business Success

KING of PENTACLES

## 1. Purpose:

This spell is designed to attract success, stability, and growth in business—whether it's your own venture or a project you want to see thrive. It helps unlock the energy of abundance and opens paths to opportunities and clients.

This ritual will help you:

-Attract success and growth in business
-Increase financial stability and commercial opportunities
-Remove blockages that hinder business progress
-Improve confidence and strategic decision-making

## 2. Optimal Moon Phase:

Waxing Moon or Full Moon: To enhance expansion, success, and abundance in business.

## 3. Materials:

-1 gold candle (success, wealth, and recognition)
-1 green candle (prosperity and financial growth)
-1 blue candle (mental clarity and business strategy)
-Cinnamon (attracts money and opportunities)
-Basil (protection and business success)
-Bay leaves (symbol of victory and business achievements)
-Sandalwood oil (prosperity and success)
-Orange oil (optimism and positive energy in business)
-Citrine (attracts wealth and success in business)
-Pyrite (magnet for opportunities and money)
-Tiger's Eye (confidence and protection in the business realm)

-Tarot card: The Emperor (leadership and stability in business)
-Tarot card: The Ace of Pentacles (new opportunities and financial growth)
-Tarot card: The Six of Wands (success, recognition, and business achievements)

## 4. Procedure:

1. Find a quiet place where you won't be disturbed. Light sandalwood or orange incense to cleanse the energy and attract success.

2. Anoint the candles with sandalwood and orange oils, from the base to the wick, visualizing prosperity and success flooding your business. Sprinkle cinnamon, bay leaves, and basil around the candles. Place the citrine, pyrite, and tiger's eye near the candles.

3. In the center, place "The Emperor" (symbolizes strength and leadership in business). To the left, place "The Ace of Pentacles" (attracts new financial opportunities). To the right, place "The Six of Wands" (represents success and recognition in the business world).

4. First, light the gold candle, saying: "Success and wealth flood my business." Then light the green candle, saying: "Prosperity flows through every area of my work." Finally, light the blue candle, saying: "Clarity and wisdom guide me to success."

5. With your hands over the tarot cards and your eyes on the candle flames, repeat with conviction: "Success surrounds me, abundance calls to me, my business thrives and my path becomes clear. Clients arrive, money flows, everything I touch turns to gold. So it is, so it shall be."

6. Close your eyes and take a deep breath. Imagine your business flourishing, with satisfied clients and money flowing

freely. Visualize steady growth and financial stability.

## 5. Closing the ritual:

1. Thank the universe for the energy of success received.

2. Write an affirmation on a piece of paper, such as:
"My business is prosperous and successful," and keep
it in the cash register or in your wallet.

3. Let the candles burn out (or extinguish them with your
fingers if you wish to repeat the ritual over several nights).

4. Carry the citrine or pyrite with you to keep the energy of
abundance active.

## 6. Duration:

The effects may be felt in the following weeks through new
opportunities and improvements in your business. You can
repeat the ritual during each waxing moon or full moon to
enhance its power.

## 7. Extra tip:

Place a bay leaf at the entrance of your business or office
to attract clients and success.

# 5.4

## Spell for Luck in Games of Chance

KING OF PENTACLES

### 1. Purpose:

This spell is designed to increase luck in games of chance, lotteries, betting, and raffles. It doesn't guarantee instant results, but it aligns your energy with fortune and prosperity, increasing the chances of success.

This ritual will help you:

-Increase luck in gambling and betting
-Attract fortune and positive energy
-Enhance intuition to make better decisions while playing
-Remove blockages that prevent the flow of good luck

### 2. Optimal Moon Phase:

Waxing Moon or Full Moon: To boost the attraction of good fortune and abundance

### 3. Materials:

-1 gold candle (represents wealth and luck)
-1 green candle (for prosperity and money)
-1 yellow candle (for positive energy and the attraction of opportunities)
-Cinnamon (attracts fortune and money)
-Basil (symbol of success and good luck)
-Bay leaves (protection and attraction of victory)
-Sandalwood oil (to enhance luck)
-Orange oil (to attract opportunities and financial success)
-Pyrite (stone of wealth and prosperity)
-Citrine (attracts money and luck in games)
-Green Aventurine (energy of winnings and success)

-Tarot card: The Wheel of Fortune (change of luck and success in chance)
-Tarot card: The Magician (ability to attract opportunities and make the right decisions)
-Tarot card: The Nine of Pentacles (abundance and unexpected gains)

## 4. Procedure:

1. Find a quiet place where you can perform the ritual without interruptions. Light cinnamon or sandalwood incense to harmonize the energy and attract luck.

2. Anoint the candles with sandalwood and orange oils, from the base to the wick, visualizing luck flowing into your life. Sprinkle cinnamon, bay leaves, and basil around the candles. Place the pyrite, citrine, and green aventurine near the candles.

3. In the center, place "The Wheel of Fortune" (to attract luck in games of chance). To the left, place "The Magician" (to enhance intuition and skill in games). To the right, place "The Nine of Pentacles" (to ensure winnings and abundance).

4. First, light the gold candle, saying: "Fortune and wealth come to me effortlessly." Then light the green candle, saying: "Money flows into my life with ease and joy." Finally, light the yellow candle, saying: "Luck is on my side in every opportunity."

5. With your hands over the tarot cards and your eyes on the candle flames, repeat with conviction: "May luck and fate turn in my favor, may fortune smile on me with radiant power. Success and abundance are on my way, wealth and prosperity will soon stay. So it is, so it shall be."

6. Close your eyes and take a deep breath. Visualize luck surrounding you, attracting money and winnings. Imagine yourself winning a game of chance or receiving an

unexpected prize.

## 5. Closing the ritual:

1. Thank the universe for the luck and abundance received.

2. Write the phrase on a piece of paper: "Luck and wealth are always with me," and keep it in your wallet or next to your lottery tickets.

3. Let the candles burn out (or extinguish them with your fingers if you wish to repeat the ritual over several nights).

4. Carry the citrine or green aventurine with you as a lucky charm.

## 6. Duration:

The effects may be felt in the following days through improved luck and better outcomes in games of chance. You can repeat the ritual during each waxing moon or full moon to enhance its power.

## 7. Extra tip:

Before playing, rub the pyrite or citrine between your hands while mentally repeating: "Luck is on my side."

# 5.5

## Spell for Promotion and Professional Recognition

KING OF PENTACLES

## 1. Purpose:

This spell is designed to attract recognition in the workplace, support a promotion, and gain the respect and admiration of colleagues and superiors. It helps strengthen confidence, remove obstacles, and open paths to professional success.

This ritual will help you:

-Obtain a promotion or career advancement
-Attract professional recognition and respect
-Increase confidence and authority at work
-Remove blockages and improve your reputation

## 2. Optimal Moon Phase:

Waxing Moon or Full Moon: To enhance expansion and progress in your professional career

## 3. Materials:

-1 gold candle (for success and authority)
-1 blue candle (for leadership and effective communication)
-1 green candle (for stability and professional growth)
-Bay leaves (symbol of triumph and recognition)
-Rosemary (protection and mental clarity at work)
-Cinnamon (attracts success and opportunities)
-Sandalwood oil (to enhance authority and presence)
-Lemon oil (for clarity and wise decision-making)
-Pyrite (attracts success, wealth, and recognition)
-Tiger's Eye (confidence and protection in the professional realm)

-Citrine (energy of leadership and prosperity)
-Tarot card: The Emperor (leadership, authority, and promotion)
-Tarot card: The Six of Wands (recognition and public success)
-Tarot card: The Ace of Pentacles (new job opportunities and stability)

## 4. Procedure:

1. Find a quiet place without interruptions. Light sandalwood or cinnamon incense to cleanse the space and attract success.

2. Anoint the candles with sandalwood and lemon oils, from the base to the wick, while visualizing recognition and success in your work. Sprinkle bay leaves, rosemary, and cinnamon around the candles. Place the pyrite, tiger's eye, and citrine near the candles.

3. In the center, place "The Emperor" (symbolizing leadership and career stability). To the left, place "The Six of Wands" (to attract recognition and success). To the right, place "The Ace of Pentacles" (symbolizing new opportunities for growth and promotion).

4. First, light the gold candle, saying: "Success and recognition are coming into my life." Then light the blue candle, saying: "My leadership and skills are valued and acknowledged." Finally, light the green candle, saying: "Stability and professional growth are mine."

5. With your hands over the tarot cards and your eyes on the candle flames, repeat with conviction: "Success is mine, triumph awaits me, my efforts are recognized, my worth is revealed. May my talent shine brightly, and my promotion arrive with prosperity. So it is, so it shall be."

6. Close your eyes and take a deep breath. Imagine your

bosses and colleagues recognizing your work and praising your skills. Visualize the moment you receive a promotion or advancement, feeling the satisfaction of achievement.

## 5. Closing the ritual:

1. Thank the universe for the energy of success received.

2. Write an affirmation on a piece of paper, such as: "I am recognized and valued at work; my success is inevitable," and keep it on your desk or in your wallet.

3. Let the candles burn out (or extinguish them with your fingers if you wish to repeat the ritual over several nights).

4. Carry the pyrite or tiger's eye with you to keep the energy of success active.

## 6. Duration:

The effects may be felt in the following weeks through increased recognition and new job opportunities.
You can repeat the ritual during each waxing moon or full moon to enhance its power.

## 7. Extra tip:

Place a bay leaf on your desk and write your professional goal on it to reinforce the energy of the spell.

# 5.6

**Spell for Unexpected Wealth**

KING OF PENTACLES

## 1. Purpose:

This spell is designed to attract unexpected money, whether through gifts, inheritances, games of chance, unforeseen opportunities, or sudden income increases. Its purpose is to open financial paths and unlock the energy of sudden abundance.

This ritual will help you:

-Attract money unexpectedly and effortlessly
-Open paths to abundance and prosperity
-Remove financial blockages that prevent wealth from arriving
-Enhance intuition to recognize financial opportunities

## 2. Optimal Moon Phase:

Waxing Moon or Full Moon: To boost the attraction of wealth and good fortune

## 3. Materials:

-1 gold candle (to attract wealth and financial success)
-1 green candle (for prosperity and financial stability)
-1 yellow candle (for luck and positive energy)
-Cinnamon (attracts money and luck)
-Bay leaves (symbolize success and fortune)
-Basil (opens financial paths and protects income)
-Sandalwood oil (to enhance wealth)
-Orange oil (to attract financial opportunities)
-Pyrite (stone of wealth and abundance)
-Citrine (attracts unexpected money and financial success)
-Green Aventurine (energy of winnings and luck)

-Tarot card: The Wheel of Fortune (positive change and unexpected wealth)
-Tarot card: The Ace of Pentacles (financial opportunities and unexpected money)
-Tarot card: The Nine of Pentacles (abundance and financial stability)

## 4. Procedure:

1. Find a quiet place without interruptions. Light sandalwood or cinnamon incense to harmonize the energy and attract abundance.

2. Anoint the candles with sandalwood and orange oils, from the base to the wick, visualizing wealth flowing toward you. Sprinkle cinnamon, bay leaves, and basil around the candles. Place the pyrite, citrine, and green aventurine near the candles.

3. In the center, place "The Wheel of Fortune" (symbolizing the arrival of unexpected wealth). To the left, place "The Ace of Pentacles" (to attract financial opportunities). To the right, place "The Nine of Pentacles" (symbolizing the enjoyment of abundance).

4. First, light the gold candle, saying: "Wealth and fortune come to me in abundance." Then light the green candle, saying: "Money flows into my life in unexpected and constant ways." Finally, light the yellow candle, saying: "Luck and prosperity are with me every day."

5. With your hands over the tarot cards and your eyes on the candle flames, repeat with conviction: "May gold and fortune arrive without delay, unexpected abundance is on its way. Money flows with no limits or strain, and wealth in my life finds its domain. So it is, so it shall be."

6. Close your eyes and take a deep breath. Imagine a golden rain of coins and bills falling over you. Visualize yourself

receiving an unexpected sum of money from an unknown source.

**5. Closing the ritual:**

1. Thank the universe for the wealth and luck received.

2. Write the amount of money you wish to receive on a piece of paper and place it under the pyrite.

3. Let the candles burn out (or extinguish them with your fingers if you wish to repeat the ritual over several nights).

4. Carry the citrine or green aventurine with you as a charm for unexpected wealth.

**6. Duration:**

The effects may be felt in the following weeks through opportunities for unexpected money. You can repeat the ritual during each waxing moon or full moon to enhance its power.

**7. Extra tip:**

Every day, look at yourself in the mirror at least once with a radiant smile and, with strong intention, recite: "Money comes to me in unexpected and abundant ways."

# 5.7

**Spell for Financial Stability**

KING OF PENTACLES

## 1. Purpose:

This spell is designed to attract financial stability, remove money blockages, and strengthen prosperity in a steady and lasting way. It focuses on securing regular income, managing expenses, and encouraging long-term financial growth.

This ritual will help you:

-Ensure stable and consistent income
-Attract prosperity and financial order
-Eliminate blockages that prevent economic stability
-Protect your finances and encourage sustained abundance

## 2. Optimal Moon Phase:

-Waxing Moon: To attract stability and financial growth
-Full Moon: To strengthen abundance and consolidate financial security

## 3. Materials:

-1 green candle (prosperity and financial growth)
-1 gold candle (success and wealth)
-1 white candle (protection and financial stability)
-Bay leaves (symbolize stability and financial success)
-Cinnamon (attracts money and constant prosperity)
-Rosemary (protection and clarity in financial decisions)
-Sandalwood oil (to attract stability and wealth)
-Peppermint oil (for clarity and financial wisdom)
-Pyrite (magnet for wealth and financial stability)

-Citrine (attracts steady income and financial success)
-Tiger's Eye (protection against financial losses and poor investments)
-Tarot card: The Emperor (represents solidity and financial control)
-Tarot card: The Four of Pentacles (symbol of stability and economic security)
-Tarot card: The Ace of Pentacles (financial opportunities and economic growth)

## 4. Procedure:

1. Find a quiet place where you can perform the ritual without interruptions. Light sandalwood or cinnamon incense to harmonize the energy and attract stability.

2. Anoint the candles with sandalwood and peppermint oils, from the base to the wick, while visualizing stability and order in your finances. Sprinkle bay leaves, cinnamon, and rosemary around the candles. Place the pyrite, citrine, and tiger's eye near the candles.

3. In the center, place "The Emperor" (to strengthen stability and financial control). To the left, place "The Four of Pentacles" (to ensure protection and financial security). To the right, place "The Ace of Pentacles" (to attract new financial opportunities).

4. First, light the white candle, saying: "I protect my finances and remove all financial blockages." Then light the gold candle, saying: "Wealth and financial success are constant in my life." Finally, light the green candle, saying: "My financial stability grows with harmony and security."

5. With your hands over the tarot cards and your eyes on the candle flames, repeat with conviction: "Abundance flows and does not cease, stability in my life holds its peace." Money arrives with order and certainty, and my finances grow with strength. So it is, so it shall be."

6. Close your eyes and take a deep breath. Imagine your bank account increasing, your income remaining steady, and your finances growing in a stable way. Visualize a golden flow of abundance surrounding you and securing your financial well-being.

## 5. Closing the ritual:

1. Thank the universe for the financial stability received.

2. Write an affirmation on a piece of paper such as: "I have financial security and stability in my life," and keep it in your wallet or on your desk.

3. Let the candles burn out (or extinguish them with your fingers if you wish to repeat the ritual over several nights).

4. Carry the pyrite or tiger's eye with you as a charm for financial stability.

## 6. Duration:

The effects may be felt in the following weeks through improved financial order and economic opportunities. You can repeat the ritual during each waxing moon or full moon to enhance its power.

## 7. Extra tip:

Keep a bay leaf in your wallet with the phrase "My finances are strong and stable," to keep the energy of the spell active.

# 5.8

## Spell to Remove Financial Blockages and Limitations

KING OF PENTACLES

## 1. Purpose:

This spell is designed to break energetic and emotional barriers that prevent the flow of money in your life. It helps release limiting beliefs, eliminate debt, and open paths to financial stability and growth.

This ritual will help you:

-Remove blockages that prevent money from coming in
-Break patterns of scarcity and financial hardship
-Open paths to prosperity and abundance
-Attract financial opportunities and stability

## 2. Optimal Moon Phase:

-Waning Moon: To eliminate blockages and negative energies
-Waxing Moon: To attract new financial opportunities

## 3. Materials:

-1 black candle (to eliminate blockages and negative energy)
-1 green candle (to attract prosperity)
-1 gold candle (for wealth and financial stability)
-Cinnamon (attracts prosperity and accelerates the manifestation of money)
-Rue (cleanses negative energies and breaks financial curses)
-Bay leaves (symbol of success and abundance)
-Sandalwood oil (to unblock financial energy)
-Peppermint oil (for clarity and opening paths)

-Black obsidian (protection and removal of energetic blockages)
-Citrine (attracts money and financial opportunities)
-Pyrite (magnet for wealth and financial stability)
-Tarot card: Death (transformation and elimination of financial blockages)
-Tarot card: The Ace of Pentacles (new economic opportunities)
-Tarot card: The Six of Pentacles (financial balance and incoming money)

## 4. Procedure:

1. Find a quiet place where you can focus. Light sandalwood or cinnamon incense to cleanse the energy in the space and attract prosperity.

2. Anoint the black candle with sandalwood oil, visualizing it absorbing and destroying all financial blockages. Anoint the green candle with peppermint oil, imagining open paths to abundance. Anoint the gold candle with both oils, sealing in the energy of success and wealth. Sprinkle cinnamon, rue, and bay leaves around the candles. Place the black obsidian, citrine, and pyrite near the candles.

3. In the center, place "Death" (symbolizing the removal of financial blockages). To the left, place "The Ace of Pentacles" (to attract new opportunities for wealth). To the right, place "The Six of Pentacles" (symbolizing financial balance and the arrival of money).

4. First, light the black candle, saying: "I break and destroy all financial blockages in my life." Then light the green candle, saying: "I open the paths to prosperity and success." Finally, light the gold candle, saying: "Money flows into my life steadily and abundantly."

5. With your hands over the tarot cards and your eyes on the candle flames, repeat with conviction: "I break the chains of

scarcity without fear today, money and abundance come my way. Nothing blocks my path, nothing stops my rise, wealth is mine and flows at all times. So it is, so it shall be."

6. Close your eyes and take a deep breath. Imagine negative energies and financial blockages dissolving in the candlelight. Visualize golden doors opening and a constant flow of money entering your life.

## 5. Closing the ritual:

1. Thank the universe for the release and the flow of abundance.

2. Write down your financial fears or blockages on a piece of paper and burn it in the black candle to destroy them.

3. Let the candles burn out (or extinguish them with your fingers if you wish to repeat the ritual over several nights).

4. Carry pyrite or citrine with you as a charm to maintain the energy of prosperity.

## 6. Duration:

The effects may be felt in the following days through improved financial flow and new opportunities. You can repeat the ritual during each waning moon (to remove blockages) and each waxing moon (to attract prosperity).

## 7. Extra tip:

Write the phrase "Abundance flows without limits in my life" on a bay leaf and keep it in your wallet or workplace.

# 6

# SPELLS FOR HEALTH AND WELL-BEING

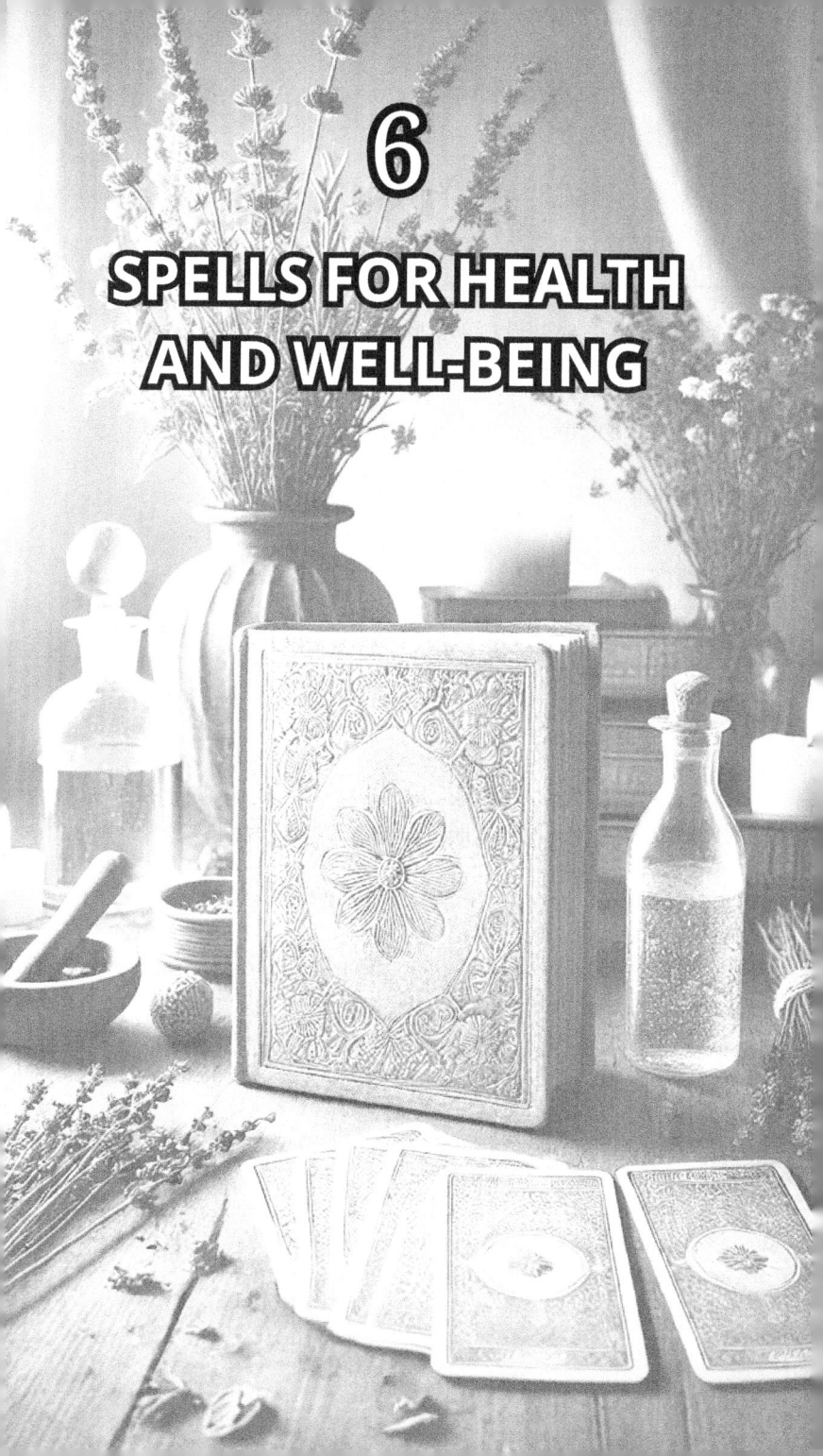

# 6.1

## Spell for Physical Healing

### 1. Purpose:

This spell is designed to support physical health recovery, promote bodily healing, and strengthen vital energy. It can be used to relieve illness, accelerate healing processes, or boost the immune system.

This ritual will help you:

-Accelerate the body's healing
-Restore balance and vital energy
-Relieve pain and improve physical well-being
-Support recovery after illness or injury

### 2. Optimal Moon Phase:

-Waxing Moon: To strengthen the body and improve health
-Full Moon: To enhance healing and regeneration

### 3. Materials:

-1 white candle (for purification and healing)
-1 blue candle (for peace and bodily harmony)
-1 green candle (for regeneration and physical health)
-Chamomile (healing and calm)
-Rosemary (purification and physical strength)
-Eucalyptus (energy renewal and relief of ailments)
-Lavender oil (relaxation and pain relief)
-Eucalyptus oil (decongestion and energy cleansing)
-Amethyst (transmutation and body balance)
-Green quartz (healing and physical strength)
-Black tourmaline (protection and removal of negative energies)

-Tarot card: Temperance (balance and recovery)
-Tarot card: The Sun (vitality and full health)
-Tarot card: Four of Swords (rest and regeneration)

## 4. Procedure:

1. Find a quiet place where you can focus. Light lavender or eucalyptus incense to purify the space and support healing.

2. Anoint the candles with lavender and eucalyptus oils, from the base to the wick, while visualizing healing energy flowing through your body. Sprinkle chamomile, rosemary, and eucalyptus around the candles. Place the amethyst, green quartz, and black tourmaline near the candles.

3. In the center, place "Temperance" (symbolizing balance and recovery). To the left, place "The Sun" (to restore vitality and health). To the right, place "The Four of Swords" (to enhance rest and regeneration).

4. First, light the white candle, saying: "The light of healing surrounds me and purifies my body." Then light the blue candle, saying: "Calm and harmony restore my well-being." Finally, light the green candle, saying: "My body grows stronger, my health is reborn with each new day."

5. With your hands over the tarot cards and your eyes on the candle flames, repeat with conviction: "Holy light, divine energy, heal my body, restore my life. Let pain dissolve, let strength return, and let health remain within me. So it is, so it shall be."

6. Close your eyes and take a deep breath. Imagine a golden light descending upon you and enveloping your entire body. Visualize every cell in your body regenerating and filling with healing energy.

## 5. Closing the ritual:

1. Thank the universe and the healing energies for their intervention.

2. Write the phrase: "My body is strong, my health is being restored" on a piece of paper and place it under your pillow.

3. Let the candles burn out (or extinguish them with your fingers if you wish to repeat the ritual over several nights).

4. Carry green quartz with you as a healing amulet.

**6. Duration:**

The effects may be felt in the following days with increased well-being and physical recovery. You can repeat the ritual during each waxing or full moon to reinforce its power.

**7. Extra tip:**

Drink a chamomile and rosemary infusion after the ritual to complement the healing process with natural properties.

# 6.2

**Spell for Energy and Vitality**

## 1. Purpose:

This spell is designed to boost physical, mental, and spiritual energy, helping to overcome tiredness, fatigue, and lack of motivation. Its purpose is to revitalize the body and mind, restoring balance and inner strength.

This ritual will help you:

-Increase energy and vitality
-Combat exhaustion and fatigue
-Enhance motivation and enthusiasm
-Revitalize body, mind, and spirit

## 2. Optimal Moon Phase:

-Waxing Moon: To increase energy and dynamism
-Full Moon: To boost strength and overall balance

## 3. Materials:

-1 red candle (for vitality and dynamism)
-1 yellow candle (for mental energy and clarity)
-1 white candle (for purification and balance)
-Ginger (boosts vitality and endurance)
-Rosemary (strengthens body and mind)
-Cinnamon (attracts positive energy and motivation)
-Eucalyptus oil (revitalization and physical strength)
-Lemon oil (mental energy and clarity)
-Carnelian (increases energy and creativity)
-Red quartz (revitalization and strength)
-Citrine (joy and motivation)
-Tarot card: The Sun (symbol of vitality and energy)

-Tarot card: The Magician (mastery over energy and potential)
-Tarot card: The Ace of Wands (new energy and action)

## 4. Procedure:

1. Find a quiet place where you can focus. Light rosemary or cinnamon incense to cleanse the energy and revitalize the space.

2. Anoint the red candle with eucalyptus oil, visualizing an explosion of energy within you. Anoint the yellow candle with lemon oil, feeling clarity and mental vitality. Anoint the white candle with both oils, asking for balance and renewal. Sprinkle ginger, rosemary, and cinnamon around the candles. Place the carnelian, red quartz, and citrine near the candles.

3. In the center, place "The Sun" (symbolizing life force and renewed energy). To the left, place "The Magician" (to enhance the ability to channel energy). To the right, place "The Ace of Wands" (to activate energy and motivation).

4. First, light the white candle, saying: "I purify my body and mind, I release exhaustion." Then light the yellow candle, saying: "My mind is clear, my energy flows freely." Finally, light the red candle, saying: "Vitality and strength are mine, I am full of energy."

5. With your hands over the tarot cards and your eyes on the candle flames, repeat with conviction: "Power of the sun, energy of the earth, my body is filled, my mind lifts high.  Every cell shines with strength and might, vitality in me is reborn in light. So it is, so it shall be."

6. Close your eyes and take a deep breath. Imagine a golden fire growing within you, filling you with energy and vitality. Visualize your body strong, active, and full of motivation.

## 5. Closing the ritual:

1. Thank the universe and the energy of the sun for the strength received.

2. Write the affirmation: "I am pure energy, my vitality grows every day" on a piece of paper and keep it in a visible place.

3. Let the candles burn out (or extinguish them with your fingers if you wish to repeat the ritual over several nights).

4. Carry the carnelian or citrine with you as a vitality amulet.

## 6. Duration:

The effects may be felt in the following days with increased energy and motivation. You can repeat the ritual during each waxing moon or full moon to enhance its power.

## 7. Extra tip:

Before starting your day, hold the carnelian in your dominant hand and repeat: "I am filled with energy and vitality."

# 6.3

XIX

THE SUN

## Spell for Emotional and Mental Balance

## 1. Purpose:

This spell is designed to harmonize the mind and emotions, dispel anxiety, calm confusion, and bring clarity. It helps to find inner stability, manage stress, and improve mental peace.

This ritual will help you:

-Balance emotions and thoughts
-Reduce anxiety and stress
-Improve mental clarity and decision-making
-Attract serenity and inner harmony

## 2. Optimal Moon Phase:

-Waning Moon: To release stress and negativity
-Waxing Moon: To strengthen calm and emotional stability

## 3. Materials:

-1 white candle (for purification and inner peace)
-1 blue candle (for serenity and emotional balance)
-1 lilac or purple candle (for mental stability and transmutation)
-Lavender (relaxation and harmony)
-Chamomile (calm and emotional clarity)
-Rosemary (protection against negative thoughts)
-Lavender oil (to reduce stress and balance emotions)
-Sandalwood oil (to center the mind and calm anxiety)
-Amethyst (for mental balance and spiritual protection)
-Rose quartz (to heal emotions and foster self-love)
-Lapis lazuli (for mental clarity and inner communication)
-Tarot card: Temperance (harmony and balance)

-Tarot card: The Hermit (clarity and inner reflection)
-Tarot card: The Star (hope and emotional healing)

## 4. Procedure:

1. Find a quiet place where you can relax without interruptions. Light lavender or sandalwood incense to purify the energy and invite calm.

2. Anoint the candles with lavender and sandalwood oils, from the base to the wick, while visualizing serenity flooding your being. Sprinkle lavender, chamomile, and rosemary around the candles. Place the amethyst, rose quartz, and lapis lazuli near the candles.

3. In the center, place "Temperance" (to restore inner harmony). To the left, place "The Hermit" (for introspection and mental clarity). To the right, place "The Star" (for emotional healing and hope).

4. First, light the white candle, saying: "Light and peace purify my mind and soul." Then light the blue candle, saying: "My heart and emotions are balanced with serenity." Finally, light the lilac candle, saying: "My mind is filled with clarity and calm."

5. With your hands over the tarot cards and your eyes on the candle flames, repeat with conviction: "Calm and balance awaken in me, my mind and soul in harmony shall be. Stress dissolves, peace surrounds, and inner clarity forever abounds. So it is, so it shall be."

6. Close your eyes and take a deep breath. Imagine a blue light surrounding your entire body, calming your mind and healing your emotions. Visualize peace and clarity settling within you, dissolving confusion and distress.

## 5. Closing the ritual:

1. Thank the universe for the mental and emotional peace received.

2. Write the affirmation: "I am peace, balance, and clarity" on a piece of paper and place it under your pillow or in a special place.

3. Let the candles burn out (or extinguish them with your fingers if you wish to repeat the ritual over several nights).

4. Carry amethyst or rose quartz with you as an emotional balance amulet.

**6. Duration:**

The effects may be felt in the following days with a greater sense of calm and stability. You can repeat the ritual during each waning or waxing moon to reinforce its power.

**7. Extra tip:**

Before going to sleep, hold the rose quartz in your hand and repeat: "I am calm, my mind and heart are in harmony."

# 6.4

**Spell for Restful Sleep**

## 1. Purpose:

This spell is designed to improve sleep quality, reduce insomnia, and eliminate energies that interfere with deep rest. It's ideal for those who suffer from stress, intrusive thoughts, or frequent awakenings at night.

This ritual will help you:

-Promote deep and restorative sleep
-Eliminate worries and tension before bedtime
-Attract peace and serenity during rest
-Protect the sleeping space from negative energies

## 2. Optimal Moon Phase:

-Waning Moon: To dispel insomnia and remove energetic blockages
-New Moon: To reset sleep cycles and renew energy

## 3. Materials:

-1 blue candle (for tranquility and rest)
-1 white candle (for purification and protection during sleep)
-Lavender (relaxation and mental calm)
-Chamomile (induces deep and peaceful sleep)
-Valerian (to ward off insomnia and stress)
-Lavender oil (relaxation and harmony)
-Sandalwood oil (to calm the mind and improve rest)
-Amethyst (reduces anxiety and protects during sleep)
-Rose quartz (harmonizes emotions before sleep)
-White howlite (dispels negative thoughts and relaxes the mind)

-Tarot card: The Moon (symbol of the dream world and subconscious)
-Tarot card: Four of Swords (rest, recovery, and relaxation)
-Tarot card: The Star (inner peace and connection with universal energy)

## 4. Procedure:

1. Find a quiet place without interruptions. Perform the ritual in your bedroom before going to sleep. You can play relaxing music or nature sounds if you wish.

2. Anoint the blue candle with lavender oil, visualizing deep and restorative rest. Anoint the white candle with sandalwood oil, asking for protection and purification of your sleeping space. Sprinkle lavender, chamomile, and valerian around the candles. Place the amethyst, rose quartz, and howlite near the candles or under your pillow.

3. In the center, place "The Moon" (to connect with deep, uninterrupted rest). To the left, place "The Four of Swords" (for relaxation and mental rest). To the right, place "The Star" (for serenity and energetic harmony).

4. First, light the white candle, saying: "I purify my space, my body, and my mind. Rest surrounds me." Then light the blue candle, saying: "Peace and tranquility are with me; my sleep is deep and restorative."

5. With your hands over the tarot cards and your eyes on the candle flames, repeat with conviction: "May calm embrace me, may the night guide me, restorative sleep now dwells within me." My thoughts grow quiet, my mind finds rest, and sleep in my life is sweet and blessed. So it is, so it shall be."

6. Close your eyes and take a deep breath. Imagine a blue light surrounding you, filling you with peace and relaxation. Visualize yourself entering deep, restorative sleep and waking up the next morning with renewed energy.

### 5. Closing the ritual:

1. Thank the universe and the energies of the night for their support.

2. Write the affirmation: "My sleep is deep and restorative every night" on a piece of paper and place it under your pillow.

3. Let the candles burn out, or extinguish them with your fingers if you wish to repeat the ritual over several nights.

4. Place the amethyst or howlite under your pillow to maintain restful energy.

### 6. Duration:

The effects may be felt that very night or in the following days, improving sleep quality and reducing restlessness. You can repeat the ritual during each waning or new moon to reinforce its power.

### 7. Extra tip:

Before going to sleep, rub a few drops of lavender oil on your wrists and take three deep breaths.

# 6.5

XIX
THE SUN

**Detox Spell**

## 1. Purpose:

This spell is designed to assist in the elimination of physical, emotional, and energetic toxins. It can be helpful for breaking harmful habits, overcoming addictions, cleansing the body and mind, and renewing vital energy.

This ritual will help you:

-Purify the body from toxins and unhealthy habits
-Release negative emotions and blocked energies
-Strengthen willpower and determination
-Promote physical and mental regeneration

## 2. Optimal Moon Phase:

-Waning Moon: To eliminate harmful habits and toxins
-New Moon: To initiate deep cleansing and renewal

## 3. Materials:

-1 white candle (for purification and renewal)
-1 green candle (for healing and regeneration)
-1 black candle (to eliminate toxins and harmful habits)
-Sage (for energetic cleansing and purification)
-Rosemary (for protection and strength)
-Dandelion (for detoxifying the body and mind)
-Eucalyptus oil (to release blockages and toxins)
-Lemon oil (for purification and mental clarity)
-Amethyst (for transmuting negative energy and purification)
-Green quartz (for regeneration and healing of the body)
-Black obsidian (for protection and removal of toxic habits)

-Tarot card: Death (transformation and removal of what is harmful)
-Tarot card: Judgment (rebirth and deep cleansing)
-Tarot card: Ace of Cups (emotional renewal and well-being)

## 4. Procedure:

1. Find a quiet place without interruptions. Light sage or rosemary incense to cleanse the energy of the space.

2. Anoint the black candle with eucalyptus oil, visualizing it absorbing and removing all toxins and negative habits from your life. Anoint the green candle with lemon oil, feeling healing and regeneration within your body. Anoint the white candle with both oils, asking for balance and total purification. Sprinkle sage, rosemary, and dandelion around the candles. Place the amethyst, green quartz, and black obsidian near the candles.

3. In the center, place "Death" (symbolizing the end of what is harmful and transformation). To the left, place "Judgment" (for renewal and deep cleansing). To the right, place "The Ace of Cups" (for emotional purification and well-being).

4. First, light the black candle, saying: "All negative energy and harmful habits dissolve and disappear." Then light the green candle, saying: "My body and mind regenerate, my health blossoms." Finally, light the white candle, saying: "I am clean, free, and in harmony with myself."

5. With your hands over the tarot cards and your eyes on the candle flames, repeat with conviction: "I leave behind what harms me, I renew my being, body and mind bloom in balance within. Toxins fade away, healing leads the way, and peace within me shines every day. So it is, so it shall be."

6. Close your eyes and take a deep breath. Imagine a white light descending over you, cleansing every cell in your body and releasing all toxins and negative habits. Visualize

yourself feeling lighter, stronger, and in harmony.

**5. Closing the ritual:**

1. Thank the universe for the cleansing and healing received.

2. Write down the habits or negative energies you wish to eliminate on a piece of paper and burn it in the black candle.

3. Let the candles burn out (or extinguish them with your fingers if you wish to repeat the ritual over several nights).

4. Carry amethyst or black obsidian with you as a protective and cleansing amulet.

**6. Duration:**

The effects may be felt in the following days with greater mental clarity and physical well-being. You can repeat the ritual during each waning moon to reinforce its power.

**7. Extra tip:**

Drink a dandelion and ginger infusion after the ritual to complement the detox with natural benefits.

# 6.6

## Spell for Spiritual Healing

THE SUN

### 1. Purpose:

This spell is designed to restore inner peace, remove negative
energetic burdens, and connect with the spiritual essence.
It helps heal deep emotional wounds, strengthen intuition,
and balance the soul's energy.

This ritual will help you:

-Heal spiritual and emotional wounds
-Remove negative energies and emotional burdens
-Align and balance the spirit with your life purpose
-Enhance the connection with intuition and divine energy

### 2. Optimal Moon Phase:

-Waning Moon: To release negative energies and heal past
wounds.
-Full Moon: To enhance spiritual connection and strengthen
the soul.

### 3. Materials:

-1 white candle (for purification and spiritual healing)
-1 blue candle (for inner peace and spiritual connection)
-1 violet candle (for energy transmutation and spiritual
elevation)
-Lavender (for harmonizing the spirit and relaxation)
-Sage (for deep cleansing and purification)
-Rue (for spiritual protection and removing blockages)
-Sandalwood oil (to raise vibration and strengthen connection
with the higher self)

-Frankincense oil (for spiritual cleansing and connection with the divine)
-Amethyst (for energy transmutation and soul healing)
-Clear quartz (for spiritual clarity and energy amplification)
-Lapis lazuli (for wisdom and connection with inner truth)
-Tarot card: The Star (hope and spiritual renewal)
-Tarot card: The Hermit (inner search and spiritual growth)
-Tarot card: Judgment (spiritual rebirth and release from the past)

## 4. Procedure:

1. Find a quiet place where you won't be disturbed. Light sandalwood incense or any incense to cleanse the space and raise its vibration.

2. Anoint the white candle with frankincense oil, visualizing the purification of your spirit. Anoint the blue candle with sandalwood oil, feeling peace and serenity flowing into your soul. Anoint the violet candle with both oils, asking for transmutation and spiritual elevation. Sprinkle lavender, sage, and rue around the candles. Place the amethyst, clear quartz, and lapis lazuli near the candles.

3. In the center, place The Star (symbolizing healing and hope). On the left, place *The Hermit* (for introspection and inner connection). On the right, place *Judgment* (for rebirth and spiritual liberation).

4. First, light the white candle, saying: "Light and purity heal my spirit, my soul is cleansed." Then light the blue candle, saying: "Peace and harmony surround me and balance my being." Finally, light the violet candle, saying: "I transmute all negativity into light and spiritual elevation."

5. With your hands over the tarot cards and your eyes on the candle flames, repeat with conviction: "Divine energy, light of the universe, heal my soul, dissolve my fear. May peace reign in my spirit, and may clarity always shine in my life.

So it is, so it shall be."

6. Close your eyes and take a deep breath. Imagine a white light descending upon you, filling you with healing energy. Visualize everything weighing on your soul dissolving into the light, making room for peace and harmony.

## 5. Closing the Ritual:

1. Thank the universe for the healing and clarity you've received.

2. Write down an affirmation such as: "I am at peace, my soul is in balance," and keep it on your altar or sacred space.

3. Let the candles burn down completely (or extinguish them with your fingers if you plan to repeat the ritual on several nights).

4. Carry the amethyst or clear quartz with you as a talisman for spiritual healing.

## 6. Duration:

The effects may be felt in the following days as greater peace, clarity, and spiritual stability. You can repeat the ritual during each waning or full moon to strengthen its power.

## 7. Extra Tip:

Before going to sleep, hold the amethyst in your hand and repeat: "I am in harmony with my spirit, my soul is at peace."

# 6.7

## Chakra Harmonization Spell

THE SUN

### 1. Purpose:

This spell is designed to balance and align the seven main chakras of the body, promoting physical, emotional, and spiritual well-being. It helps remove energy blockages, improve the flow of vital energy, and enhance inner harmony.

This ritual will help you:

-Balance and harmonize the chakras
-Remove energetic blockages and restore energy flow
-Improve physical, emotional, and spiritual health
-Align personal energy with universal vibration

### 2. Optimal Moon Phase:

-Full Moon: To enhance energy and strengthen inner balance
-Waxing Moon: To activate and revitalize the chakras

### 3. Materials:

-Red candle (Root chakra – stability and security)
-Orange candle (Sacral chakra – creativity and emotions)
-Yellow candle (Solar plexus chakra – personal power and confidence)
-Green candle (Heart chakra – love and harmony)
-Light blue candle (Throat chakra – communication and expression)
-Indigo candle (Third eye chakra – intuition and wisdom)
- Violet candle (Crown chakra – spiritual connection)
-Ginger root (to activate vital energy)
-Lavender (for peace and harmonization)
-Sage (to clear energetic blockages)

-Frankincense oil (to raise vibration and awareness)
-Sandalwood oil (to stabilize energy)
-Red jasper (root chakra)
-Carnelian (sacral chakra)
-Citrine (solar plexus chakra)
-Green quartz (heart chakra)
-Lapis lazuli (throat chakra)
-Amethyst (third eye chakra)
-Clear quartz (crown chakra)
-Tarot card: The World (balance and energetic fulfillment)
-Tarot card: The Magician (connection and control of inner energy)
-Tarot card: The Star (harmony and energy flow)

## 4. Procedure:

1. Find a quiet place where you can focus without interruptions. Light lavender or sandalwood incense to purify the space and raise its vibration.

2. Anoint each candle with frankincense and sandalwood oil, visualizing how each one connects with its corresponding chakra. Sprinkle the herbs (sage, lavender, and ginger) around the candles. Place the stones aligned in the order of the chakras, from root to crown.

3. In the center, place The World (symbolizing total harmonization). On the left, place The Magician (to enhance control of energy). On the right, place The Star (to ensure flow and well-being).

4. Light the candles in ascending order, from red to violet. As you light each one, visualize its color radiating energy into its corresponding chakra.

5. With your hands over the tarot cards and your gaze on the candle flames, repeat with conviction: "Universal energy, source of life, may it flow through my body pure and divine. From the root to the vast sky, I harmonize my chakras with

love and direction. So it is, so it shall be."

6. Close your eyes and take a deep breath. Imagine a stream of light flowing through your body, aligning and activating each chakra. Feel the energy moving freely, balancing your entire being.

## 5. Closing the Ritual:

1. Thank the universe for the healing and balance you have received.

2. Write down the affirmation: "My energy is in balance, my chakras are aligned" and keep it in your sacred space.

3. Let the candles burn down completely (or extinguish them with your fingers if you wish to repeat the ritual over several nights).

4. Carry the amethyst or clear quartz with you to maintain energetic balance.

## 6. Duration:

The effects may be felt in the days that follow as greater mental clarity, emotional stability, and physical well-being. You can repeat the ritual during each full or waxing moon to reinforce its power.

## 7. Extra Tip:

Each morning upon waking, visualize each chakra glowing with its corresponding color and repeat: "My energy flows in harmony, my being is balanced."

# 6.8

## Spell for Addiction Healing

### 1. Purpose:

This spell is designed to assist in the release of addictions and harmful habits, strengthening willpower, mental clarity, and the healing of body and mind. It focuses on breaking negative patterns, removing blockages, and attracting renewing and balancing energy.

This ritual will help you:

-Break free from dependence on substances or addictive behaviors
-Strengthen willpower and determination
-Heal the body, mind, and spirit from the effects of addiction
-Replace negative habits with positive and constructive energies

### 2. Optimal Moon Phase:

-Waning Moon: To eliminate addiction and break dependency
-New Moon: To begin a new stage free of attachments

### 3. Materials:

-1 black candle (to eliminate addiction and cut negative energy)
-1 white candle (for purification and healing)
-1 green candle (for physical and mental recovery)
-Rue (removes negative energy and harmful influences)
-Sage (for energetic cleansing and protection)
-Rosemary (for strength and mental clarity)
-Lavender oil (to calm anxiety and stabilize the mind)
-Eucalyptus oil (to purify and release energetic toxins)

-Amethyst (for transmutation of negative energy and impulse control)
-Black obsidian (for protection and breaking harmful patterns)
-Green quartz (for healing and physical recovery)
-Tarot card: Death (transformation, end of addiction, and rebirth)
-Tarot card: Judgment (release and firm decision to change)
-Tarot card: Ace of Swords (mental clarity and willpower)

## 4. Procedure:

1. Find a quiet place where you can concentrate without interruptions. Light sage or sandalwood incense to cleanse the space and remove negative energies.

2. Anoint the black candle with eucalyptus oil, visualizing it absorbing and destroying the energy of addiction. Anoint the white candle with lavender oil, feeling purification and inner peace. Anoint the green candle with both oils, asking for recovery and balance. Sprinkle rue, sage, and rosemary around the candles. Place the amethyst, black obsidian, and green quartz near the candles.

3. In the center, place Death (symbolizing the end of addiction and transformation). On the left, place Judgment (to make the decision to change and free yourself). On the right, place Ace of Swords (for mental clarity and determination).

4. First, light the black candle, saying: "Today I break the chains of addiction; what binds me fades away." Then light the white candle, saying: "My body and mind are purified; peace and light surround me." Finally, light the green candle, saying: "I am strong, healthy, and free. The energy of life renews me."

5. With your hands over the tarot cards and your eyes on the candle flames, repeat with conviction: "Today I release the past and heal my being. My will is strong, my spirit is powerful. What binds me dissolves into light, and my path

is clear, free, and pure. So it is, so it shall be."

6. Close your eyes and take a deep breath. Imagine a golden light surrounding you and dissolving any ties to addiction. Visualize yourself as a free, strong, and peaceful person in harmony with yourself.

## 5. Closing the Ritual:

1. Thank the universe for the strength and healing you've received.

2. Write down what you wish to leave behind and burn it in the black candle to symbolize its release.

3. Let the candles burn down completely (or extinguish them with your fingers if you plan to repeat the ritual on multiple nights).

4. Carry the amethyst or black obsidian with you as a talisman of protection and willpower.

## 6. Duration:

The effects may be felt in the days that follow as increased mental clarity and better control over impulses. You can repeat the ritual during each waning moon until you feel completely free from addiction.

## 7. Extra Tip:

Each morning, hold the amethyst in your hand and repeat: "I am free, my will is strong, my life is in balance."

# 7

# PROTECTION AND DEFENSE SPELLS

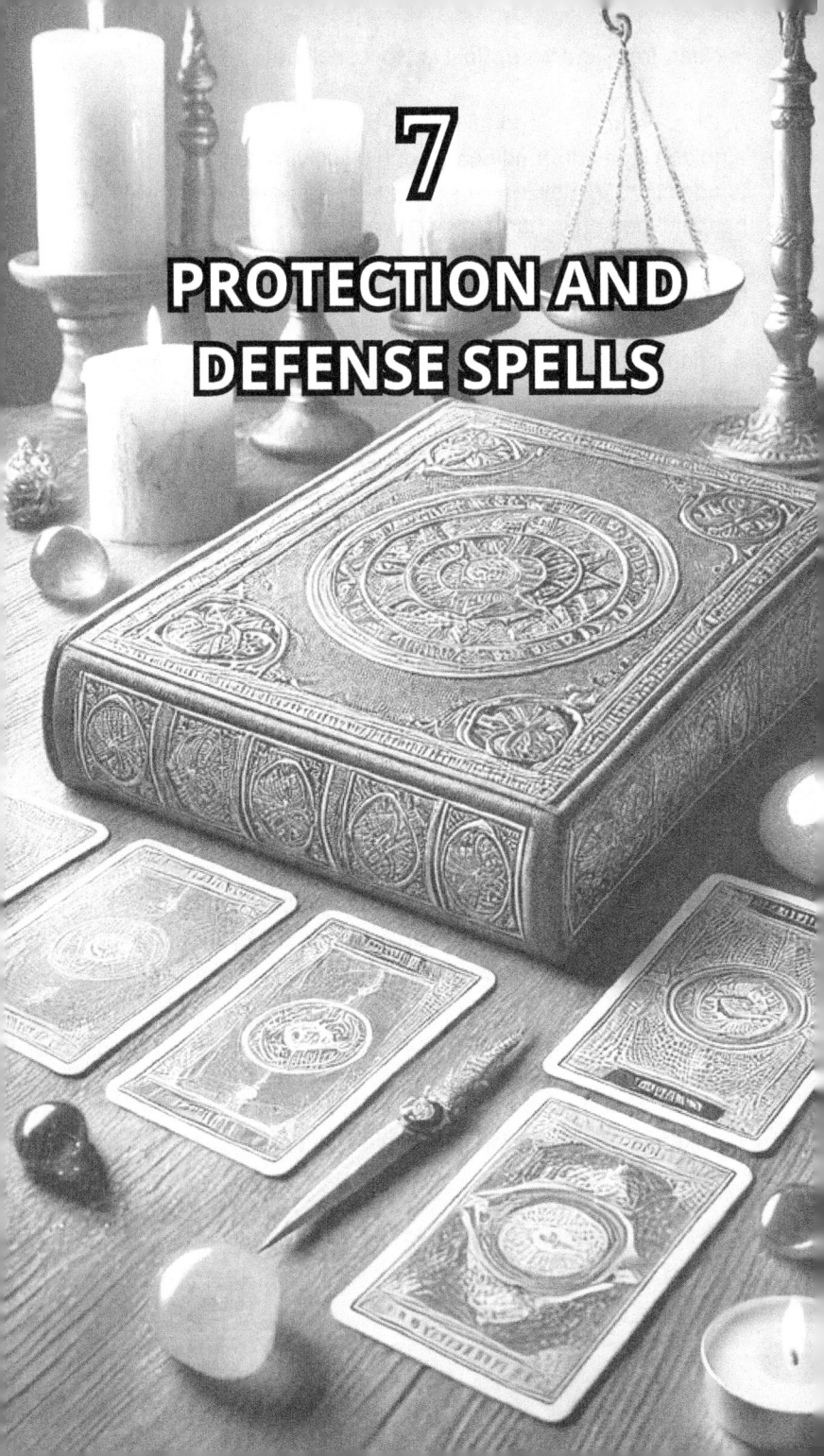

# 7.1

**Spell for Personal Protection**

XI

JUSTICE

## 1. Purpose:

This spell is designed to create a protective energetic shield against negative energies, harmful influences, psychic attacks, and any form of spiritual harm. It is ideal for strengthening the aura and generating a field of safety and balance.

This ritual will help you:

-Protect yourself from negative energies and ill intentions
- Strengthen your aura and personal balance
-Eliminate psychic attacks and harmful vibrations
-Increase your sense of security and self-confidence

## 2. Optimal Moon Phase:

-Waning Moon: To dispel and remove negative energies
-Waxing Moon: To strengthen the protective shield

## 3. Materials:

-1 black candle (to absorb and dispel negative energies)
-1 white candle (for purification and divine protection)
-1 blue candle (for stability and calm)
-Rue (for protection against negativity)
-Rosemary (for purification and energetic strength)
-Bay leaves (for defense and success)
-Sandalwood oil (to enhance protective energy)
-Eucalyptus oil (to remove negative burdens)
-Black obsidian (for protection against psychic attacks and harmful energies)
-Black tourmaline (to absorb negativity and reinforce the aura)

-Clear quartz (to amplify protection and clarity)
-Tarot card: The Tower (to dissolve any threat or negativity)
-Tarot card: The Magician (for mastery of personal energy
and protection)
-Tarot card: The Sun (for strength and security)

## 4. Procedure:

1. Find a quiet place where you can focus without
interruptions. Light rue or sandalwood incense to
cleanse the space and drive away negative energies.

2. Anoint the black candle with eucalyptus oil, visualizing it
absorbing and neutralizing any negative energy. Anoint the
white candle with sandalwood oil, feeling divine light and
protection surrounding you. Anoint the blue candle with
both oils, asking for stability and inner peace. Sprinkle rue,
rosemary, and bay leaves around the candles. Place the
black obsidian, tourmaline, and clear quartz near the candles.

3. In the center, place The Tower (to dissolve threats and
eliminate negativity). On the left, place The Magician (to
empower yourself and strengthen your protection). On
the right, place The Sun (to radiate security and strength).

4. First, light the black candle, saying: "All negative energy
disappears; nothing harmful can reach me." Then light the
white candle, saying: "Light surrounds me; divine protection
guides me." Finally, light the blue candle, saying: "My spirit
is strong; my aura is a shield of power."

5. With your hands over the tarot cards and your eyes on
the candle flames, repeat with conviction: "I am free and
protected from all shadow; no evil can touch my reflection.
Light and strength dwell within me; my shield is strong,
unbreakable it shall be. So it is, so it shall be."

6. Close your eyes and take a deep breath. Imagine a golden
sphere of light surrounding you, growing stronger and more

impenetrable. Visualize any negative energy moving away and dissolving into nothingness.

## 5. Closing the Ritual:

1. Thank the universe for the protection you have received.

2. Write down the affirmation: "I am protected at all times; my energy is strong and secure" and keep it in your wallet or a sacred space.

3. Let the candles burn down completely (or extinguish them with your fingers if you wish to repeat the ritual over several nights).

4. Carry black tourmaline or obsidian with you as a protective talisman.

## 6. Duration:

The effects may be felt in the following days as a heightened sense of security and energetic stability. You can repeat the ritual during each waning or waxing moon to strengthen its power.

## 7. Extra Tip:

Each morning, touch your protective talisman and repeat: "My energy is protected, my light is unbreakable."

# 7.2

## Spell for Home Protection

JUSTICE

### 1. Purpose:

This spell is designed to safeguard the home from negative energies, bad influences, envy, or any force that may disturb the peace of the space. It will create a protective barrier and ensure a harmonious and safe environment.

This ritual will help you:

-Protect the house from negative energies and bad influences
-Create a protective shield against envy and ill intentions
-Purify the home and attract peace and harmony
-Strengthen the home's positive energy and security

### 2. Optimal Lunar Phase:

-Waning Moon: To remove negative energies and cleanse the home
-Waxing or Full Moon: To strengthen the protection and stability of the home

### 3. Materials:

-1 white candle (for purification and protective light)
-1 blue candle (for stability and peace in the home)
-1 black candle (to dispel and absorb negative energies)
-Rue (protection against bad energies and envy)
-Rosemary (cleansing and harmonizing the space)
-Bay leaf (protective shield and success in the home)
-Sandalwood oil (for energetic protection of the space)
-Lavender oil (for peace and tranquility in the home)

-Black tourmaline (absorbs negative energies and protects the home)
-Amethyst (harmonizes and purifies the energy of the environment)
-Clear quartz (amplifies protection and energetic clarity)
-Tarot card: The Tower (to dissolve any threat or negative energy in the home)
-Tarot card: The Magician (to empower the protective energy)
-Tarot card: The World (to ensure stability and peace in the home)

## 4. Procedure:

1. Physically clean the home before the ritual (you can sweep or mop with water and salt). Light rue, rosemary, or sandalwood incense to purify the space. Turn off artificial lights and work with candlelight.

2. Anoint the white candle with lavender oil, visualizing a white light surrounding the home. Anoint the blue candle with sandalwood oil, asking for peace and stability in the home. Anoint the black candle with both oils, asking it to absorb all negative energy. Sprinkle rue, rosemary, and bay leaf around the candles. Place the black tourmaline, amethyst, and clear quartz near the candles.

3. In the center, place The Tower (to dissolve any threat or negative energy in the home). To the left, place The Magician (to empower the protective energy). To the right, place The World (to ensure stability and peace in the home).

4. First, light the black candle, saying: "All shadow and ill intent dissolve, my home is clean and protected." Then light the white candle, saying: "Light and peace dwell in my house, harmony is strengthened." Finally, light the blue candle, saying: "My home is a safe refuge, no harm can reach it."

5. With your hands over the tarot cards and your eyes on the candle flames, repeat with conviction: "May the light guard my

door, may peace reign in every corner, my home is protected, no darkness enters it. So it is, so it shall be."

6. Close your eyes and take a deep breath. Imagine your home surrounded by a bubble of golden and white light, protecting it from any harm. Visualize all negative energy leaving and disappearing.

## 5. Closing the Ritual:

1. Give thanks to the universe for the protection and stability of your home.

2. Write the affirmation "My home is safe, protected, and filled with peace" on a piece of paper and place it near the main door.

3. Let the candles burn down (or extinguish them with your fingers if you plan to repeat the ritual over several nights).

4. Place the black tourmaline near the door to continue protecting the home.

## 6. Duration:

The effects may be felt in the following days as increased peace and protection in the home. You can repeat the ritual during each waning moon (to eliminate negativity) or waxing/full moon (to reinforce protection).

## 7. Extra Tip:

To maintain protective energy, place a sprig of rosemary and bay leaf at your home's entrance and replace it every month.

# 7.3

### Spell for Protection Against Envy
### and the Evil Eye

XI
JUSTICE

## 1. Purpose:

This spell is designed to block and dispel negative energies
sent through envy, the evil eye, or harmful intentions
from others. It will create a protective shield around
you, preventing any bad energy from affecting you.

This ritual will help you:

-Block the evil eye and harmful intentions
-Protect against envy and negative energies
-Create a protective shield around your aura
-Keep away people with bad intentions

## 2. Optimal Lunar Phase:

-Waning Moon: To remove any accumulated negative energy
-Waxing Moon: To strengthen protection and repel envy

## 3. Materials:

-1 black candle (to absorb negativity and break the evil eye)
-1 white candle (for purification and protection)
-1 blue candle (for stability and inner peace)
-Rue (to remove the evil eye and envy)
-Rosemary (to cleanse negative energies and protect the
aura)
-Bay leaf (to block bad energy and attract success)
-Sandalwood oil (to create a protective barrier)
-Eucalyptus oil (to dispel bad energies and clear the aura)
-Tiger's eye (protection against envy and the evil eye)

-Black tourmaline (absorbs negativity and blocks energetic attacks)
-Amethyst (spiritual protection and energy transmutation)
-Tarot card: The Moon (to reveal and dispel hidden ill intentions)
-Tarot card: The Devil (to break energetic ties and envy)
-Tarot card: The Sun (to illuminate and strengthen protection)

## 4. Procedure:

1. Find a quiet place where you won't be disturbed. Light rue or sandalwood incense to cleanse the space and remove any lingering negative energy.

2. Anoint the black candle with eucalyptus oil, visualizing it absorbing and neutralizing any evil eye or envy. Anoint the white candle with sandalwood oil, feeling purity and protection surrounding you. Anoint the blue candle with both oils, asking for peace and balance in your life. Sprinkle rue, rosemary, and bay leaf around the candles. Place the tiger's eye, black tourmaline, and amethyst near the candles.

3. In the center, place The Moon (to reveal and dispel hidden energies). To the left, place The Devil (to break negative influences and cut envy). To the right, place The Sun (to radiate protection and strength).

4. First, light the black candle, saying: "All envy and bad energy fade and break." Then light the white candle, saying: "Light surrounds me, purity protects me." Finally, light the blue candle, saying: "I am at peace, my energy is strong and unbreakable."

5. With your hands over the tarot cards and your eyes on the candle flames, repeat with convictio: "No envy can touch me, no evil eye can harm me. I am protected by light and love, my energy is strong, nothing will affect me. So it is, so it shall be."

6. Close your eyes and take a deep breath. Imagine a golden light surrounding you, forming an impenetrable shield of protection. Visualize any negative energy bouncing off and dissolving into nothingness.

## 5. Closing the Ritual:

1. Give thanks to the universe for the protection received.

2. Write the affirmation "I am protected from all envy and the evil eye" on a piece of paper and keep it in your wallet or in a sacred space.

3. Let the candles burn down (or extinguish them with your fingers if you plan to repeat the ritual over several nights).

4. Carry the tiger's eye or black tourmaline with you as a protective charm.

## 6. Duration:

The effects may be felt in the following days with a greater sense of peace and protection. You can repeat the ritual during each waning or waxing moon to reinforce its power.

## 7. Extra Tip:

To strengthen protection, place a bay leaf and a sprig of rue at the entrance of your home or inside your bag.

# 7.4

## Spell to Dispel Astral Parasites, Implanted Devices, and Dark Entities

### 1. Purpose:

This spell is designed to eliminate any astral parasites, energetic implants, or dark entities that may be draining your energy or interfering with your spiritual growth. Its purpose is to cut cords, cleanse the aura, and restore your energetic protection.

This ritual will help you:

-Dissolve and expel astral parasites and dark entities
-Remove energetic implants that drain your energy
-Restore balance to the aura and reconnect with the light
-Create a protective shield to prevent further interference

### 2. Optimal Lunar Phase:

-Waning Moon: To expel entities, implants, and astral parasites
-New Moon: To begin a new cycle of protection and clean energy

### 3. Materials:

-1 black candle (to absorb and eliminate entities and astral parasites)
-1 white candle (to purify and restore light to the aura)
-1 violet candle (to transmute energies and cut cords)
-White sage (to purify the aura and dispel entities)
-Rue (to cut ties with dark energies)
-Wormwood (to repel negative influences and astral parasites)
-Sandalwood oil (to raise vibration and dissolve energetic

implants)
-Lavender oil (to restore peace and protection to the aura)
-Black obsidian (for protection and cutting energetic ties with dark entities)
-Amethyst (for spiritual energy cleansing and transmutation)
-Clear quartz (for restoring clarity and energetic balance)
-Tarot card: The Tower (to destroy and eliminate astral interference)
-Tarot card: The Hermit (to find guidance and light in spiritual healing)
-Tarot card: Judgement (for the release of dark energies and the recovery of personal power)

## 4. Procedure:

1. Find a quiet place where you can perform the ritual without interruptions. Light white sage or sandalwood incense to purify the space. Keep the lights off and use only candlelight.

2. Anoint the black candle with sandalwood oil, visualizing it absorbing and destroying any astral parasites or energetic implants. Anoint the violet candle with lavender oil, feeling it transmute and remove interference. Anoint the white candle with both oils, asking it to restore purity and peace in your aura. Sprinkle sage, rue, and wormwood around the candles. Place the black obsidian, amethyst, and clear quartz near the candles.

3. In the center, place The Tower (to destroy entities and energetic blockages). To the left, place The Hermit (to guide your spiritual cleansing process). To the right, place Judgement (for release and energetic renewal).

4. First, light the black candle, saying: "All parasites, dark entities, and astral implants are now dissolved and removed." Then light the violet candle, saying: "Negative energy is transmuted into light, my aura is restored." Finally, light the white candle, saying: "I am light, I am protection, my being is clean and in balance."

5. With your hands over the tarot cards and your eyes on the candle flames, repeat with conviction: "By the light that dwells within me, by the power of sacred fire, I break all bonds, I cut all ties, and I expel from my being what is not mine.""May all shadow dissolve, may all interference vanish—my body and spirit are free. So it is, so it shall be."

6. Close your eyes and take a deep breath. Imagine a violet light descending over you, moving through your body and eliminating any energetic implant or astral parasite. Visualize those energies dissolving into nothingness as your being fills with golden light.

## 5. Closing the Ritual:

1. Thank the universe for the release and protection received.

2. Write the affirmation: "I am free from all interference, my energy is mine and mine alone" on a piece of paper and burn it in the black candle.

3. Let the candles burn down (or extinguish them with your fingers if you plan to repeat the ritual over several nights).

4. Carry black obsidian or amethyst with you as a protective amulet.

## 6. Duration:

The effects may be felt in the following days as increased mental clarity, renewed energy, and a feeling of lightness. You can repeat the ritual during each waning or new moon to strengthen its power.

## 7. Extra tip:

To maintain your protection, cleanse your aura with a bath of salt and rue every week, and place an obsidian stone under your pillow while you sleep.

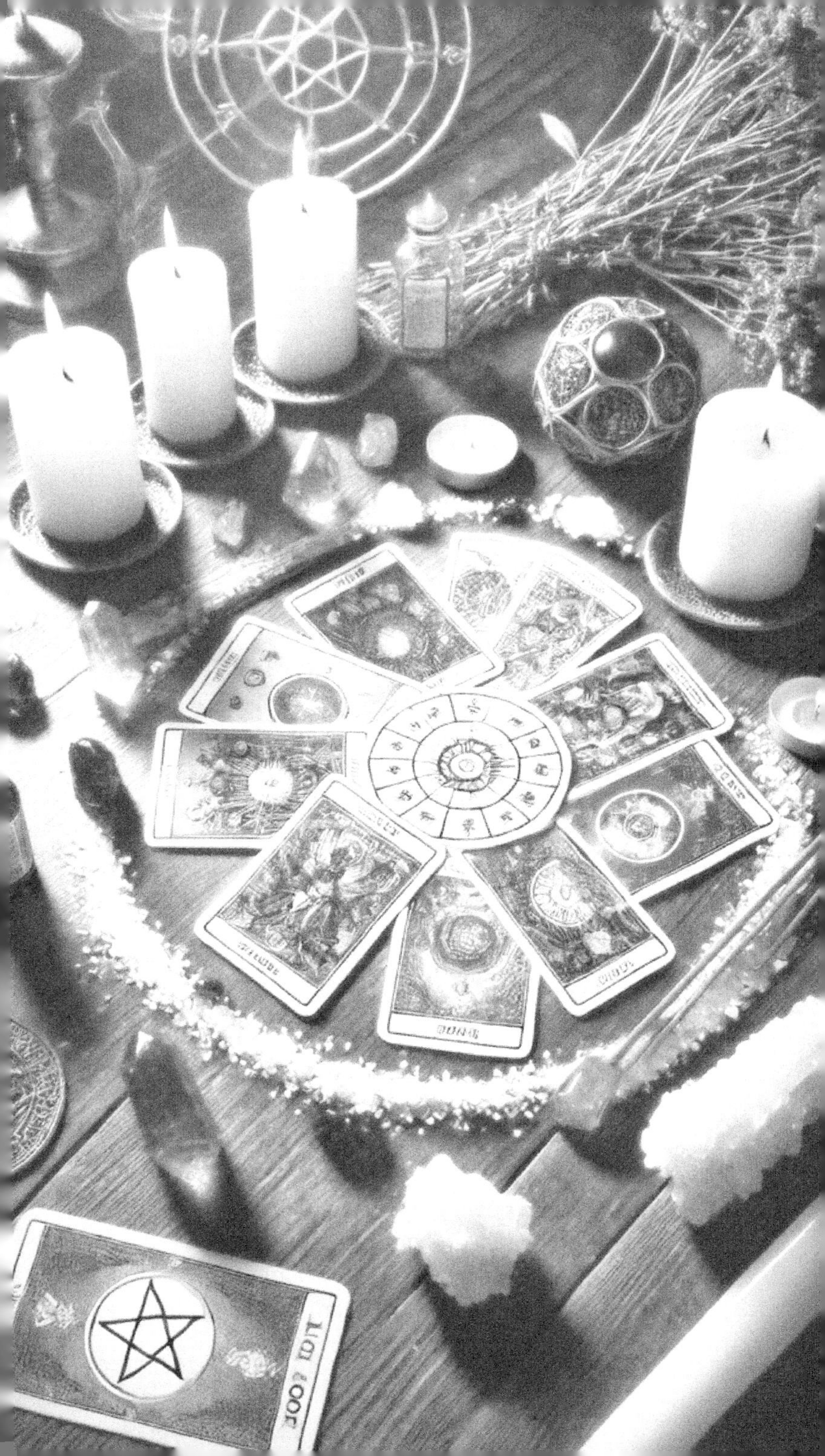

# 7.5

## Spell to Elevate Souls
## or Attached Disembodied Beings

XI
JUSTICE

## 1. Purpose:

This spell is designed to help souls trapped on the earthly plane find peace and ascend to the light. It is useful when you feel the presence of a spirit attached to a place or person and wish to release it with love and compassion.

This ritual will help you:

-Release souls or disembodied beings trapped on the earthly plane
-Guide spirits toward the light with love and peace
-Cleanse residual energies and close open spiritual portals
-Leave a space of protection and harmony after the elevation

## 2. Optimal Lunar Phase:

-Waning Moon: To assist in the detachment and release of the spirit
-Full Moon: To illuminate its path toward transcendence

## 3. Materials:

-1 white candle (for peace and the soul's elevation)
-1 blue candle (for spiritual healing and comfort)
-1 violet candle (for the soul's transmutation and release)
-Lavender (to calm and lovingly guide the spirit)
-Sage (to purify the space and remove residual energies)
-Rue (to close any portal and prevent new attachments)
-Frankincense oil (to raise spiritual vibration)
-Myrrh oil (to aid in the spirit's transition)
-Amethyst (for the soul's transmutation and guidance)

-Clear quartz (to channel pure light to the spirit)
-Selenite (to facilitate connection with the higher spiritual dimension)
-Tarot card: Judgement (soul's release and ascension)
-Tarot card: The Star (hope, light, and spiritual guidance)
-Tarot card: Death (transformation and passage to another plane)

## 4. Procedure:

1. Find a quiet place and light frankincense or myrrh incense to purify the environment. If you perform the ritual in a home where you feel the presence of the spirit, open the windows to allow energy to circulate. Maintain an attitude of respect, love, and compassion toward the soul you wish to elevate.

2. Anoint the white candle with frankincense oil, visualizing a light illuminating the spirit's path. Anoint the blue candle with myrrh oil, asking for peace and healing for the soul. Anoint the violet candle with both oils, imagining the process of transmutation and release. Sprinkle lavender, sage, and rue around the candles. Place the amethyst, clear quartz, and selenite near the candles.

3. In the center, place Judgement (for the soul's release and ascension). On the left, place The Star (to guide with light and hope). On the right, place Death (to support the spiritual transition).

4. First, light the white candle, saying: "May peace and light surround you, wandering soul, your path to eternity now opens." Then light the blue candle, saying: "May healing come to you, may love and calm guide you toward your destiny." Finally, light the violet candle, saying: "All earthly ties dissolve, you are free to follow your path into the light."

5. With your hands over the tarot cards and your gaze on the candle flames, repeat with compassion: "Wandering soul,

beloved soul, your time here has come to an end. May the divine light guide you, and may your journey be sacred. Nothing binds you anymore, nothing holds you back. I release you with love, with peace and faith. May your spirit ascend to its home, where rest and happiness await you. So it is, so it shall be."

6. Close your eyes and take a deep breath. Imagine a great golden light descending and wrapping the disembodied soul in love and peace. Visualize how it says goodbye with gratitude and rises into the light, free from all earthly burdens.

## 5. Closing the Ritual:

1. Give thanks to the universe and to the spiritual energies for their guidance and assistance.

2. Write on a piece of paper the affirmation: "This soul has found its path, love and peace accompany it," and burn it in the flame of the violet candle.

3. Let the candles burn down completely (or extinguish them with your fingers if you wish to repeat the ritual over several nights).

4. Place the selenite in the space where you felt the presence to seal the energetic portal.

## 6. Duration:

The effects may be felt in the following days as a greater lightness in the environment and the absence of energetic presences. You can repeat the ritual during each waning moon or full moon to help more souls transcend.

## 7. Extra tip:

After the ritual, cleanse your space with a sage smudge and place a glass of water with salt at your home's entrance for

3 nights to absorb any remaining energy.

# 7.6

**Spell for Protection
Against Psychic Attacks**

## 1. Purpose:

This spell is designed to block and dispel any psychic attack, energetic manipulation, or energy drainage. It creates a shield of defense around the aura, preventing entities, people, or negative energies from affecting the mind, spirit, and body.

This ritual will help you:

-Block psychic attacks and prevent energetic manipulation
-Cut ties with people or entities that drain your energy
-Strengthen the aura and psychic resilience
-Create a protective shield against negative influences

## 2. Optimal Lunar Phase:

-Waning Moon: To eliminate negative energies and cut harmful influences
-Waxing Moon: To reinforce protection and strengthen the energetic shield

## 3. Materials:

-1 black candle (to absorb and dispel psychic attacks)
-1 white candle (to purify and restore personal energy)
-1 blue candle (to reinforce the protective shield and psychic stability)
-Rue (for protection and blocking external energies)
-White sage (for purification and removal of negative influences)
-Rosemary (for spiritual and mental strength)
-Oils: Sandalwood oil (for psychic protection and

mental fortitude)
-Lavender oil (to calm the mind and seal in energy)
-Stones or Crystals: Black tourmaline (blocks psychic attacks and protects the aura)
-Amethyst (transmutes negative energy and raises vibration)
-Hematite (strengthens the mind and returns negative energy to its source)
-Tarot card: The Tower (to destroy any existing psychic attack)
-Tarot card: The Magician (to reinforce control over personal energy)
-Tarot card: The World (to ensure balance and protection within the aura)

## 4. Procedure:

1. Find a quiet place without interruptions. Light sage or sandalwood incense to cleanse the space. Turn off artificial lights and work only by candlelight.

2. Anoint the black candle with sandalwood oil, visualizing it absorbing and eliminating any psychic attack. Anoint the white candle with lavender oil, feeling the purity and restoration of your energy. Anoint the blue candle with both oils, asking for protection and stability. Sprinkle rue, sage, and rosemary around the candles. Place the black tourmaline, amethyst, and hematite near the candles.

3. In the center, place The Tower (to eliminate and dispel any psychic attack). On the left, place The Magician (to strengthen control over your energy). On the right, place The World (to ensure long-term stability and protection).

4. First, light the black candle, saying: "All ill-intentioned energy is broken and returned to its source." Then light the white candle, saying: "My aura is purified, the light restores me. "Finally, light the blue candle, saying: "I am protected by a shield of power—nothing can affect me."

5. With your hands over the tarot cards and your eyes on the candle flames, repeat with conviction: "No evil can cross my shield, no shadow can touch me. My mind is strong, my spirit shines, all negative energy dissolves and retreats." "Light is my armor, fire is my sword—no psychic attack can reach me. So it is, so it shall be."

6. Close your eyes and take a deep breath. Imagine a bluish light surrounding you, creating an impenetrable shield of protective energy. Visualize any attack bouncing off and vanishing into nothingness.

## 5. Closing the Ritual:

1. Thank the universe for the protection received.

2. Write on a piece of paper the affirmation: "I am protected from all psychic attacks, my aura is strong and secure," and place it under your pillow or in your sacred space.

3. Let the candles burn out completely (or extinguish them with your fingers if you plan to repeat the ritual over several nights).

4. Carry black tourmaline or hematite with you as a protective amulet.

## 6. Duration:

The effects may be felt in the following days as a stronger sense of safety, emotional and mental stability. You can repeat the ritual during each waning or waxing moon to reinforce its power.

## 7. Extra Tip:

To reinforce your protection, take a bath with sea salt and rosemary once a week and place a black tourmaline near your bed.

# 7.7

## Spell for Travel Protection

XI
JUSTICE

### 1. Purpose:

This spell is designed to ensure safety and well-being during travels, whether short or long. It helps prevent setbacks, accidents, theft, or any negative energy that might interfere with the travel experience.

This ritual will help you:

-Protect the traveler from accidents, setbacks, and dangers
-Ensure a smooth and obstacle-free journey
-Guard against theft, loss, and negative energies
-Maintain mental clarity and direction along the way

### 2. Optimal Lunar Phase:

-Waxing Moon: To attract good luck and protection during the trip
-Full Moon: To enhance safety and harmony throughout the journey

### 3. Materials:

-1 white candle (for protection and clarity along the path)
-1 blue candle (for calmness and safety during the journey)
-1 gold candle (to attract good luck throughout the trip)
-Bay leaves (for protection and success in travel)
-Rosemary (to prevent accidents and reinforce mental clarity)
-Cinnamon (to attract luck and positive energy along the way)
-Sandalwood oil (to strengthen energetic protection)
-Lemon oil (for clarity and to avoid confusion during the trip)
-Tiger's eye (for protection and clarity on the road)

-Black tourmaline (protection against negative energies and accidents)
-Amethyst (peace and harmony during the trip)
-Tarot card: The Chariot (to ensure a successful and smooth journey)
-Tarot card: The Star (to attract guidance and protection along the way)
-Tarot card: The Magician (to maintain control and clarity throughout the journey)

## 4. Procedure:

1. Find a quiet place and light sandalwood or rosemary incense to cleanse the space. Place the protective stones near the candles. Have a personal object ready that you will take with you on your trip (it can be a medal, a bracelet, or a small pouch with herbs).

2. Anoint the white candle with sandalwood oil, visualizing a light surrounding your path with protection. Anoint the blue candle with lemon oil, asking for calm and clarity during the trip. Anoint the gold candle with both oils, attracting good luck and success along the way. Sprinkle bay leaves, rosemary, and cinnamon around the candles.

3. In the center, place The Chariot (to ensure a safe and successful journey). On the left, place The Star (to attract guidance and protection). On the right, place The Magician (to maintain control and clarity on the path).

4. First, light the white candle, saying: "The light guides me, my path is protected." Then light the blue candle, saying: "Peace and calm accompany me every step of the way." Finally, light the gold candle, saying: "Luck and safety are on my side during this journey."

5. With your hands over the tarot cards and your eyes on the candle flames, repeat with conviction: "May my path be safe, may the light guide me, and may no shadow touch me."

"May protection surround me, and may my return be safe and blessed. The earth sustains me, the air propels me, the water grants me vision, and the fire illuminates me. Nothing will harm me, nothing will stop me. So it is, so it shall be."

6. Close your eyes and take a deep breath. Imagine a blue light wrapping around you, protecting you like a shield throughout the journey. Visualize the trip being safe, smooth, and free of obstacles.

## 5. Closing the Ritual:

1. Thank the universe for the protection and safety granted during the journey.

2. Charge the personal object (bracelet, medal, pouch of herbs) with the energy of the ritual by holding it in your hands while saying: "This amulet protects me with every step I take."

3. Let the candles burn out completely (or extinguish them with your fingers if you plan to repeat the ritual over several nights before the trip).

4. Take the consecrated object and one of the protective stones (tiger's eye or black tourmaline) with you on your journey.

## 6. Duration:

The effects can be felt from the beginning of the journey until your return. You can repeat the ritual before every important trip to reinforce protection.

## 7. Extra Tip:

Before leaving for your trip, repeat the affirmation:
"My path is safe, my journey is protected, I return in peace."

# 7.8

## Spell for Breaking Curses and Enchantments

### 1. Purpose:

This spell is designed to break any curse, negative spell, or enchantment that may be affecting your life. It helps release magical bindings, cut harmful energetic ties, and restore personal energy, returning control over your destiny.

This ritual will help you:

-Dissolve curses and break negative spells
-Cut harmful energetic ties with people or entities
-Restore personal energy and protection
-Seal the aura to prevent future magical interference

### 2. Optimal Lunar Phase:

-Waning Moon: To eliminate the influence of curses and enchantments
-New Moon: To begin a new phase free of magical bindings

### 3. Materials:

-1 black candle (to absorb and eliminate the curse or spell)
-1 white candle (to purify and restore energy)
-1 red candle (to cut energetic ties and reinforce protection)
-Rue (to break curses and ward off negative energies)
-White sage (to cleanse and purify the aura)
-Bay leaves (to close negative paths and attract protection)
-Sandalwood oil (to raise vibration and block interference)
-Eucalyptus oil (to cut magical bindings and cleanse the spirit)
-Black obsidian (for protection and breaking energetic ties)
-Hematite (to strengthen willpower and deflect negative

energies)
-Amethyst (to transmute dark energies into light)
-Tarot card: The Tower (to destroy the curse and
dissolve its influence)
-Tarot card: Judgement (for spiritual release and rebirth)
-Tarot card: The Magician (to regain power and control
over one's energy)

## 4. Procedure:

1. Find a quiet place where you can perform the ritual
without interruptions. Light white sage or sandalwood
incense to cleanse the space. Sit in the center of your
ritual area with the candles and other items around you.

2. Anoint the black candle with eucalyptus oil, visualizing
it absorbing the negative energy of the curse or spell. Anoint
the white candle with sandalwood oil, feeling it fill you with
light and purity. Anoint the red candle with both oils, asking
for the strength to cut any harmful energetic ties. Sprinkle
rue, sage, and bay leaves around the candles. Place the
black obsidian, hematite, and amethyst near the candles.

3. In the center, place The Tower (to destroy the curse
and eliminate its influence). On the left, place Judgement
(to free the soul from magical bindings). On the right,
place The Magician (to reclaim power over your destiny).

4. First, light the black candle, saying: "Every tie, every
shadow, every binding now dissolves." Then light the
white candle, saying: "The light returns to me, my
energy is purified." Finally, light the red candle,
saying: "I break every spell, I shatter every curse,
I am free."

5. With your hands over the tarot cards and your eyes on the
candle flames, repeat with conviction: "By the flame, by the
light, by the fire that purifies, I break every binding, and my
energy is cleansed. What was cast is returned, what was

imposed is dissolved. Nothing binds me, nothing touches me, my being is free, my path is unblocked. So it is, so it shall be."

6. Close your eyes and take a deep breath. Imagine a dark energy being absorbed by the black candle and dissolving into the air. Visualize a white light surrounding you and sealing any gaps in your aura. Feel every negative tie breaking and disappearing.

## 5. Closing the Ritual:

1. Thank the universe for the release and protection received.

2. Write on a piece of paper the affirmation: "I am free from all curses and spells; my energy is mine and mine alone." and burn it in the black candle.

3. Let the candles burn out completely (or extinguish them with your fingers if you wish to repeat the ritual over several nights).

4. Carry black obsidian or hematite with you as a protective amulet.

## 6. Duration:

The effects may be felt in the following days as greater mental clarity, a sense of release, and inner peace. You may repeat the ritual during each waning moon until you feel completely free of the curse or enchantment.

## 7. Extra Tip:

-Purification Bath: After the ritual, take a bath with sea salt and rue to reinforce the energetic cleansing. It is recommended to do this for at least 7 days. You can extend the process to 21 days, though it is most effective if done for 40 consecutive days.

-Protective Amulet: Carry an amethyst or hematite with you to prevent new magical influences.

-Energetic Sealing: Draw a protection symbol (such as a pentagram or the Algiz rune) on a piece of paper and place it under your pillow.

# 8

# SPELLS FOR SUCCESS AND ACHIEVEMENT

# 8.1

## Spell for Confidence and Security

THE CHARRIOT

### 1. Purpose:

This spell is designed to strengthen self-esteem, eliminate insecurity, and enhance self-confidence. It helps to overcome fears, reinforce determination, and attract positive energy to make decisions with confidence.

This ritual will help you:

-Increase self-confidence and personal security.
-Eliminate doubts, blockages, and inner fears.
-Boost willpower and clarity in decision-making.
-Attract respect and recognition from others.

### 2. Optimal Moon Phase:

-Waxing Moon: To increase confidence and personal power.
-Full Moon: To consolidate security and manifest a strong presence.

### 3. Materials:

-1 yellow candle (for mental clarity and confidence)
-1 orange candle (for personal empowerment)
-1 red candle (for strength and determination)
-Cinnamon (for security and personal energy)
-Rosemary (for protection and mental strength)
-Bay leaf (for success and confidence in decision-making)
-Sandalwood oil (to enhance self-esteem and security)
 Bergamot oil (to eliminate fear and shyness)
-Tiger's eye (for self-confidence and courage)
-Citrine (to attract positive energy and personal security)
-Hematite (for strength and emotional stability)

-Tarot card: The Emperor (for personal power and security)
-Tarot card: The Sun (for confidence and inner light)
-Tarot card: The Magician (for mastery of skills and self-confidence)

**4. Procedure:**

1. Find a quiet place and light sandalwood or rosemary incense to cleanse the space. Turn off artificial lights and work only with candlelight. Sit with your back straight, in a confident posture, feeling the power of your energy.

2. Anoint the yellow candle with sandalwood oil, visualizing clarity and security entering you. Anoint the orange candle with bergamot oil, feeling your personal empowerment. Anoint the red candle with both oils, strengthening your determination and courage. Sprinkle cinnamon, rosemary, and bay leaf around the candles. Place the tiger's eye, citrine, and hematite near the candles.

3. In the center, place "The Emperor" (to symbolize authority and self-assurance). To the left, place "The Sun" (to attract confidence and optimism). To the right, place "The Magician" (to manifest your talents and abilities).

4. First, light the yellow candle, saying: "My mind is clear, my confidence is strong." Then light the orange candle, saying: "My personal power grows with each passing day." Finally, light the red candle, saying: "I am brave, I am strong, nothing can stop me."

5. With your hands over the tarot cards and your eyes on the candle flames, repeat with conviction: "The light within me shines with power, I walk with confidence, unafraid to fall. Strength in my voice, certainty in my steps, confidence in my mind, I create my destiny. The fire gives me strength, the sun guides me, the power within me shines brighter each day. I am confident, strong, and radiant—my confidence is firm, powerful, and shining. So it is, so it shall be."

5. Close your eyes and breathe deeply. Imagine a golden light surrounding you, filling you with power and security. Visualize yourself in situations where you act with confidence and determination.

## 5. Closing the Ritual:

1. Thank the universe for the confidence and power you have received.

2. Write the affirmation on a piece of paper: "I am confident, strong, and capable of achieving everything I set my mind to." Keep it in your wallet or in a special place.

3. Let the candles burn out (or extinguish them with your fingers if you wish to repeat the ritual over several nights).

4. Carry the tiger's eye or citrine with you as a personal confidence charm.

## 6. Duration:

The effects may be felt in the following days, with greater mental clarity, elevated self-esteem, and more confidence in decision-making. You can repeat the ritual during each waxing or full moon to reinforce its power.

## 7. Extra Tip:

Before an important situation, touch your charm and repeat: "I am powerful, my energy shines, my confidence is unshakable."

# 8.2

## Spell for Overcoming Obstacles

THE CHARRIOT

## 1. Purpose:

This spell is designed to help you overcome blockages, eliminate difficulties, and attract solutions to move forward in any area of your life. It brings strength, determination, and mental clarity to face challenges and continue successfully.

This ritual will help you:

-Eliminate blockages and overcome challenges in any area of life
-Increase determination, courage, and clarity for decision-making
-Attract opportunities and open closed paths
-Protect against energies that hinder progress

## 2. Optimal Moon Phase:

-Waxing Moon: To strengthen determination and attract solutions
-Full Moon: To enhance success and remove resistance

## 3. Materials:

-1 red candle (for strength, action, and determination)
-1 yellow candle (for mental clarity and problem-solving)
-1 white candle (to purify and align energy)
-Bay leaf (for victory and success in overcoming obstacles)
-Rosemary (for protection and mental strength)
-Cinnamon (to speed up solutions and attract opportunities)
-Sandalwood oil (to unblock paths and increase confidence)
-Eucalyptus oil (to clear obstacles and negative energies).
-Tiger's eye (for determination and courage).

-Hematite (for resilience and personal power).
-Citrine (to attract solutions and maintain a positive mindset).
-Tarot card: The Wheel of Fortune (to attract opportunities and positive changes).
-Tarot card: The Chariot (to move forward with determination and success).
-Tarot card: The Tower (to break through blockages and eliminate what hinders progress).

## 4. Procedure:

1. Find a quiet place and light sandalwood or rosemary incense to cleanse the space. Sit with your back straight, feeling your energy ready to overcome any barrier.

2. Anoint the red candle with sandalwood oil, visualizing your determination igniting. Anoint the yellow candle with eucalyptus oil, sensing your path becoming clear. Anoint the white candle with both oils, ensuring any negativity is removed. Sprinkle bay leaf, cinnamon, and rosemary around the candles. Place the tiger's eye, hematite, and citrine near the candles.

3. In the center, place "The Wheel of Fortune" (to attract positive changes and opportunities). On the left, place "The Chariot" (to move forward with determination). On the right, place "The Tower" (to eliminate blockages and destroy obstacles).

4. First, light the white candle, saying: "All that holds me back dissolves, my path is cleared." Then light the yellow candle, saying: "Clarity and solutions come to me with ease." Finally, light the red candle, saying: "My determination is unstoppable, I overcome every obstacle."

5. With your hands over the tarot cards and your eyes on the candle flames, repeat with conviction: "Strength in my mind, power in my being, no obstacle can stop me. Like the river that flows without fear, my path is clear, firm, and sincere.

Nothing holds me back, nothing traps me, my destiny unfolds with success. What once blocked my way now steps aside, letting me move forward. So it is, so it shall be."

6. Close your eyes and take a deep breath. Imagine a wall in front of you and visualize it breaking apart, revealing a clear path. Feel the confidence and certainty that you can overcome any challenge.

## 5. Closing the ritual:

1. Give thanks to the universe for the energy received.

2. Write the affirmation: "I overcome all obstacles with ease and success." on a piece of paper and place it in your wallet or in a special place.

3. Let the candles burn out (or extinguish them with your fingers if you plan to repeat the ritual over several nights).

4. Carry the tiger's eye or citrine with you as a personal empowerment amulet.

## 6. Duration:

The effects may be felt in the following days with increased determination, clarity, and problem-solving ability. You can repeat the ritual during each waxing or full moon to reinforce its power.

## 7. Extra tip:

Before facing a challenge, touch your amulet and repeat: "I am stronger than any obstacle, nothing can stop me."

# 8.3

## Spell for Success in Projects

THE CHARRIOT

### 1. Purpose:

This spell is designed to enhance the energy of a project, whether it is work-related, academic, creative, or personal. It helps attract opportunities, remove blockages, strengthen confidence, and ensure everything flows successfully and gains recognition.

This ritual will help you:

-Attract success and prosperity in personal or professional projects
-Eliminate obstacles and facilitate the achievement of goals.
-Increase creativity, determination, and mental clarity
-Boost manifestation energy so the project results in a positive outcome

### 2. Optimal Lunar Phase:

-Waxing Moon: To enhance the growth and development of the project
-Full Moon: To solidify achievements and reach success in your goal

### 3. Materials:

-1 gold candle (to attract success and abundance to the project)
-1 yellow candle (for mental clarity and wise decision-making)
-1 green candle (for the growth and stability of the project)
-Bay leaf (for success and victory)
-Cinnamon (to attract opportunities and accelerate results)

-Rosemary (for protection and strength in carrying out the project)
-Sandalwood oil (to attract success and prestige in the project)
-Orange oil (to boost creativity and motivation)
-Pyrite (to attract wealth and prosperity in the project)
-Citrine (to foster creativity, confidence, and optimism)
-Tiger's eye (for determination and clarity in decision-making)
-Tarot card: The Sun (for clarity, success, and recognition)
-Tarot card: The Magician (for manifestation and control over destiny)
-Tarot card: The Wheel of Fortune (to attract opportunities and positive changes)

## 4. Procedure:

1. Find a quiet place where you can perform the ritual without interruptions. Light sandalwood or cinnamon incense to raise the energy and cleanse the space. If you have documents or representations of the project (such as sketches, contracts, or written ideas), place them near the altar.

2. Anoint the gold candle with sandalwood oil, visualizing success and abundance flowing into your project. Anoint the yellow candle with orange oil, feeling clarity and creativity energizing the process. Anoint the green candle with both oils, ensuring the project's growth and stability. Sprinkle bay leaf, cinnamon, and rosemary around the candles. Place the pyrite, citrine, and tiger's eye near the candles.

3. In the center, place "The Sun" (to illuminate the path and ensure success). Place "The Magician" on the left (to manifest resources and skills). Place "The Wheel of Fortune" on the right (to attract opportunities and prevent blockages).

4. First, light the gold candle, saying: "Success and prosperity shine upon my project." Then light the yellow candle, saying: "Clarity and wisdom guide every step I take." Finally, light the green candle, saying: "My project grows with strength and

stability."

5. With your hands over the tarot cards and your eyes on the candle flames, repeat with conviction: "Success and triumph are on my path, all I begin becomes divine. Each step is steady, each idea shines, my project grows, my goal is fulfilled. Nothing stops me, everything aligns, doors open, luck walks with me. By the strength of fire and the light of the sun, my destiny is success, my mission is honor. So it is, so it shall be."

6. Close your eyes and take a deep breath. Imagine your project completed successfully and recognized by all. Feel the satisfaction, abundance, and growth that come from your achievement.

## 5. Closing the ritual:

1. Thank the universe for the energy received.

2. Write the affirmation: "My project is successful, prosperous, and recognized." on a piece of paper and place it in your wallet or in a special place.

3. Let the candles burn out (or extinguish them with your fingers if you plan to repeat the ritual over several nights).

4. Carry the citrine or tiger's eye with you as a success amulet for your project.

## 6. Duration:

The effects may be felt in the following days with greater mental clarity, new opportunities, and progress in the project. You can repeat the ritual during each waxing or full moon to reinforce its power.

## 7. Extra tip:

Before each important step in your project, touch your amulet and repeat: "My path is full of opportunities, my project is a success."

# 8.4

**Spell for Academic Success**

## 1. Purpose:

This spell is designed to enhance concentration, memory, and mental clarity, making learning easier and supporting success in studies, exams, projects, or any academic challenge.

This ritual will help you:

-Improve concentration and information retention
-Attract success in exams, presentations, and projects
-Eliminate mental blockages and reduce academic anxiety
-Boost intelligence and mental clarity

## 2. Optimal Lunar Phase:

-Waxing Moon: To enhance learning and intellectual growth
-Full Moon: To maximize information retention and achieve success in tests or exams

## 3. Materials:

-1 yellow candle (for mental clarity and knowledge)
-1 blue candle (for concentration and calm)
-1 white candle (for protection and balance)
-Rosemary (for memory and mental clarity)
-Cinnamon (for success and quick thinking)
-Bay leaf (for victory and academic recognition)
-Peppermint oil (for focus and concentration)
-Lavender oil (for calm and stress relief)
-Citrine (for intelligence and motivation)
-Amethyst (for clarity and mental control)
-Tiger's eye (for confidence and determination)

-Tarot card: The Magician (for intellectual ability and the manifestation of success)
-Tarot card: The Sun (for success, clarity, and confidence)
-Tarot card: The World (for completion and achievement of academic goals)

## 4. Procedure:

1. Find a quiet place where you can perform the ritual without interruptions. Light peppermint or lavender incense to cleanse the space and enhance concentration. Place books, notes, or any study materials near the altar to infuse them with the energy of success.

2. Anoint the yellow candle with peppermint oil, visualizing your mind becoming more agile and receptive. Anoint the blue candle with lavender oil, feeling concentration and calm surround you. Anoint the white candle with both oils, ensuring that any mental blockages dissolve. Sprinkle rosemary, cinnamon, and bay leaf around the candles. Place the citrine, amethyst, and tiger's eye near the candles.

3. In the center, place "The Magician" (to enhance intelligence and skills). On the left, place "The Sun" (to attract clarity and success in your studies). On the right, place "The World" (to solidify academic achievements).

4. First, light the yellow candle, saying: "Wisdom and knowledge flow into my mind." Then light the blue candle, saying: "Concentration and calm guide me in my studies." Finally, light the white candle, saying: "My academic path is clear, successful, and bright."

5. With your hands over the tarot cards and your eyes on the candle flames, repeat with conviction: "My mind is strong, clear, and bright, each lesson I absorb with instant insight." Nothing stops me, I understand everything, my academic success is now mine. Wisdom flows through my being, knowledge is my power. I overcome exams and studies,

for my mind is a great path. So it is, so it shall be."

6. Close your eyes and take a deep breath. Imagine a golden light entering your mind, illuminating all your ideas and thoughts. Visualize knowledge being stored with ease and yourself succeeding in every exam or test.

## 5. Closing the ritual:

1. Thank the universe for the energy received.

2. Write the affirmation: "I learn with ease, my mind is powerful, and my academic success is guaranteed." on a piece of paper and place it on your desk or in your study notebook.

3. Let the candles burn out (or extinguish them with your fingers if you plan to repeat the ritual over several nights).

4. Carry the citrine or tiger's eye with you as an academic success amulet.

## 6. Duration:

The effects may be felt in the following days with increased focus, easier learning, and more confidence in your studies. You can repeat the ritual during each waxing or full moon to reinforce its power.

## 7. Extra tip:

Before studying or taking an exam, touch your amulet and repeat: "My mind is sharp, my knowledge is solid, my success is inevitable."

# 8.5

## Spell for Social Recognition

### 1. Purpose:

This spell is designed to attract recognition from others, increase popularity, improve reputation, and project a strong, charismatic image. It is ideal for those who wish to stand out at work, on social media, in social circles, or in any setting where external validation is important.

This ritual will help you:

-Attract recognition and respect from others
-Enhance charisma and personal influence
-Eliminate blockages that prevent you from shining socially
-Improve how others perceive you

### 2. Optimal Lunar Phase:

-Waxing Moon: To increase presence and charisma
-Full Moon: To manifest recognition and social success

### 3. Materials:

-1 gold candle (to attract success and recognition)
-1 yellow candle (for charisma and good communication)
-1 white candle (to harmonize social energy)
-Cinnamon (to attract attention and likability)
-Bay leaf (for victory and prestige)
-Rosemary (to strengthen confidence and presence)
-Jasmine oil (to boost social attraction and energetic beauty)
-Orange oil (for joy and likability)
-Pyrite (for success and magnetic attraction)
-Citrine (for self-confidence and positive energy)
-Tiger's eye (for charisma and personal security)

-Tarot card: The Sun (for fame, joy, and recognition)
-Tarot card: The World (for social projection and popularity)
-Tarot card: The Star (for influence and magnetic attraction)

## 4. Procedure:

1. Find a quiet place where you can perform the ritual without interruptions. Light jasmine or cinnamon incense to attract positive energy and raise the vibration.

2. Anoint the gold candle with jasmine oil, visualizing yourself shining with success and recognition. Anoint the yellow candle with orange oil, feeling your charisma expand. Anoint the white candle with both oils, ensuring harmony and social acceptance. Sprinkle cinnamon, bay leaf, and rosemary around the candles. Place the pyrite, citrine, and tiger's eye near the candles.

3. In the center, place "The Sun" (to illuminate your image and attract admiration). On the left, place "The World" (to enhance projection and social impact). On the right, place "The Star" (to boost personal magnetism).

4. First, light the gold candle, saying: "Success and fame walk with me, my presence shines." Then light the yellow candle, saying: "My charisma is strong, my communication is powerful." Finally, light the white candle, saying: "Harmony and recognition flow toward me."

5. With your hands over the tarot cards and your eyes on the candle flames, repeat with conviction: "Like the sun shining in the sky, my presence glows and lingers in every eye. My voice is clear, my light is bright, I attract respect, fortune, and light." Doors open, the world sees me, my name echoes, my spirit shines. I am recognized, I will be admired, and I carry the energy of success with me always. So it is, so it shall be."

6. Close your eyes and take a deep breath. Imagine the

people around you looking at you with admiration and respect. Visualize your social success, feeling confidence and charisma in every interaction.

## 5. Closing the ritual:

1. Thank the universe for the energy received.

2. Write the affirmation: "I am admired, respected, and recognized in everything I do." Keep it in your bag or in a special place.

3. Let the candles burn out (or extinguish them with your fingers if you plan to repeat the ritual over several nights).

4. Carry the citrine or tiger's eye with you as an amulet of charisma and recognition.

## 6. Duration:

The effects may be felt in the following days with increased confidence, smoother interactions, and social recognition. You can repeat the ritual during each waxing or full moon to reinforce its power.

## 7. Extra tip:

Before important meetings, events, or key interactions, touch your amulet and repeat: "My light shines, my charisma attracts, my presence leaves a mark."

# 8.6

**Spell to Enhance Personal Power**

## 1. Purpose:

This spell is designed to strengthen self-esteem, determination, and the ability to influence the world around you. It will help you reclaim your energy, remove internal blockages, and manifest your will with confidence and strength.

This ritual will help you:

-Increase confidence and inner power
-Unlock hidden potential and willpower
-Eliminate external influences that drain personal energy
-Enhance the manifestation of desires and goals

## 2. Optimal Lunar Phase:

-Waxing Moon: To boost personal power and magnetism
-Full Moon: To strengthen manifestation and leadership

## 3. Materials:

-1 red candle (for strength, courage, and action)
-1 gold candle (for success and manifestation)
-1 white candle (for harmonizing and protecting personal energy)
-Cinnamon (for energy and personal magnetism)
-Ginger (for determination and strength)
-Rosemary (for aura protection and mental clarity)
-Sandalwood oil (to raise energetic vibration and leadership)
-Orange oil (for confidence and creativity)
-Tiger's eye (for confidence, courage, and determination)
-Hematite (for stability and control over personal energy)

-Amethyst (for transmuting blockages and protecting personal power)
-Tarot card: The Emperor (for authority, control, and confidence)
-Tarot card: The Magician (for the manifestation of power and self-sufficiency)
-Tarot card: Strength (for resilience, bravery, and determination)

**4. Procedure:**

1. Find a quiet place where you can perform the ritual without interruptions. Light sandalwood or cinnamon incense to raise the energy.

2. Anoint the red candle with sandalwood oil, visualizing your energy igniting with strength and determination. Anoint the gold candle with orange oil, feeling your success and confidence grow. Anoint the white candle with both oils, ensuring protection and energetic balance. Sprinkle cinnamon, ginger, and rosemary around the candles. Place the tiger's eye, hematite, and amethyst near the candles.

3. In the center, place "The Emperor" (for authority and self-confidence). On the left, place "The Magician" (for the manifestation of personal power). On the right, place "Strength" (for courage and determination).

4. First, light the red candle, saying: "The fire within me ignites, my will is unbreakable." Then light the gold candle, saying: "Abundance and personal power flow to me." Finally, light the white candle, saying: "My energy is protected, my essence is strong."

5. With your hands over the tarot cards and your eyes on the candle flames, repeat with conviction: "The flame of power within me ignites, my voice is firm, my will cannot be broken. Nothing limits me, I manifest all that I desire, because I am

strength, because I am the master of my destiny. The world listens, the universe responds, my light shines, my essence expands. I am strong, I am free, I am invincible. So it is, so it shall be."

6. Close your eyes and take a deep breath. Imagine a golden sphere of light expanding from your solar plexus (your center of personal power). Visualize all energetic blockages dissolving and your energy growing stronger.

**5. Closing the ritual:**

1. Thank the universe for the energy received.

2. Write the affirmation: "My power is strong, my will is firm, I achieve everything I desire." Keep it in a special place.

3. Let the candles burn out (or extinguish them with your fingers if you plan to repeat the ritual over several nights).

4. Carry the tiger's eye or hematite with you as a personal power amulet.

**6. Duration:**

The effects may be felt in the following days with increased confidence, determination, and clarity in decision-making. You can repeat the ritual during each waxing or full moon to reinforce its power.

**7. Extra tip:**

Before situations that require confidence and leadership, touch your amulet and repeat: "I am strong, I am a leader, my power flows without limits."

# 8.7

## Spell for Motivation and Discipline

THE CHARRIOT

## 1. Purpose:

This spell is designed to enhance willpower, eliminate procrastination, and boost the energy needed to achieve goals. It helps maintain consistency in studies, work, healthy habits, or any personal objective.

This ritual will help you:

-Increase motivation to start and follow through with projects
-Strengthen discipline and consistency
-Eliminate internal blockages and laziness
-Provide energy and focus to achieve goals

## 2. Optimal Lunar Phase:

-Waxing Moon: To enhance motivation and personal growth
-Full Moon: To strengthen discipline and determination

## 3. Materials:

-1 red candle (for energy, action, and willpower)
-1 yellow candle (for mental clarity and focus)
-1 orange candle (for motivation and creative drive)
-Cinnamon (for energy and enthusiasm)
-Rosemary (for clarity and mental focus)
-Bay leaf (for victory and success in goals)
-Peppermint oil (to activate the mind and increase concentration)
-Sandalwood oil (for stability and discipline)
-Tiger's eye (for determination and courage)
-Hematite (for discipline and energy control)
-Citrine (for motivation and optimism)

-Tarot card: The Chariot (for drive, determination, and moving forward without distractions)
-Tarot card: The Magician (for the ability to take action and manifest goals)
-Tarot card: Strength (for discipline, endurance, and self-control)

## 4. Procedure:

1. Find a quiet place where you can perform the ritual without interruptions. Light peppermint or rosemary incense to activate the mind and energy.

2. Anoint the red candle with peppermint oil, visualizing your energy rising. Anoint the yellow candle with sandalwood oil, feeling clarity and focus enter you. Anoint the orange candle with both oils, ensuring steady motivation. Sprinkle cinnamon, rosemary, and bay leaf around the candles. Place the tiger's eye, hematite, and citrine near the candles.

3. In the center, place The Chariot (to symbolize determined progress). On the left, place The Magician (to enhance action and the ability to bring ideas to life). On the right, place Strength (to ensure discipline and consistency).

4. First, light the red candle, saying: "Energy drives me, my strength is activated." Then light the yellow candle, saying: "My mind is clear, my focus is strong." Finally, light the orange candle, saying: "Motivation guides me, my discipline is unbreakable."

5. With your hands over the tarot cards and your eyes on the candle flames, repeat with conviction: "Nothing stops me, I achieve it all, my will is strong, my steps are alive. The goal is near, the path is clear, my discipline is strong, my destiny is sacred. The fire ignites my strength and courage, every day with consistency, without fear. Nothing distracts me, nothing leads me astray, my determination shines and shows me the way. So it is, so it shall be."

6. Close your eyes and take a deep breath. Imagine a golden light surrounding you, filling you with energy and discipline. Visualize each goal being achieved with satisfaction and success.

## 5. Closing the ritual:

1. Thank the universe for the energy received.

2. Write the affirmation: "I am consistent, disciplined, and motivated. Everything I set my mind to, I achieve." and keep it on your desk or in your workspace.

3. Let the candles burn out (or extinguish them with your fingers if you plan to repeat the ritual over several nights).

4. Carry the tiger's eye or citrine with you as an amulet of discipline and motivation.

## 6. Duration:

The effects may be felt in the following days with increased energy, discipline, and determination to move forward with your goals. You can repeat the ritual during each waxing or full moon to reinforce its power.

## 7. Extra tip:

Before working on your goals or studying, touch your amulet and repeat: "My energy is steady, my discipline is unbreakable, my motivation leads me to success."

# 8.8

### Spell for Creativity and Inspiration

THE CHARRIOT

## 1. Purpose:

This spell is designed to unblock creativity, stimulate inspiration, and attract new ideas for artistic, literary, musical, or any form of creative expression. It also helps eliminate mental blocks and strengthen confidence in your own creativity.

This ritual will help you:

-Unblock creativity and attract inspiration
-Eliminate creative blocks and fear of self-expression
-Enhance originality and the flow of ideas
-Improve mental clarity and imagination

## 2. Optimal Lunar Phase:

-Waxing Moon: To boost creativity and idea development
-Full Moon: To maximize inspiration and manifest creative projects

## 3. Materials:

-1 light blue candle (for inspiration and intuition)
-1 orange candle (for creativity and expression)
-1 yellow candle (for mental clarity and creative confidence)
-Cinnamon (to enhance creativity and attract new ideas)
-Lavender (to calm the mind and open intuition)
-Bay leaf (for success in creative projects)
-Jasmine oil (to awaken inspiration and imagination)
-Bergamot oil (to boost creative confidence)
-Amethyst (for intuition and connection with imagination)
-Citrine (for creativity and positive energy)

-Lapis lazuli (for communication and artistic expression)
-Tarot card: The Star (for inspiration, creativity, and flow of ideas)
-Tarot card: The Magician (for manifestation and creative skill)
-Tarot card: The Empress (for artistic expression and creative abundance)

## 4. Procedure:

1. Find a quiet place and light jasmine or lavender incense to relax the mind. Keep creative tools nearby (pencils, brushes, instruments, notebooks, etc.).

2. Anoint the blue candle with jasmine oil, visualizing inspiration flowing through you. Anoint the orange candle with bergamot oil, feeling your creativity ignite. Anoint the yellow candle with both oils, ensuring clarity and confidence in your expression. Sprinkle cinnamon, lavender, and bay leaf around the candles. Place the amethyst, citrine, and lapis lazuli near the candles.

3. In the center, place The Star (for inspiration and creative flow). On the left, place The Magician (to activate creative abilities). On the right, place The Empress (to enhance artistic expression and abundant creativity).

4. First, light the blue candle, saying: "Inspiration flows through me, my mind is open to new ideas." Then light the orange candle, saying: "My creativity is infinite, each idea manifests with ease." Finally, light the yellow candle, saying: "I trust in my talent, my creativity shines brightly."

5. With your hands over the tarot cards and your eyes on the candle flames, repeat with conviction: "The divine spark within me ignites the light of my inspiration. Ideas flow, my art shines, my creativity is pure manifestation. Clear mind, agile hands, everything I imagine, I can create. The muses guide me, the universe inspires me, my talent blossoms, nothing can stop it. So it is, so it shall be."

6. Close your eyes and take a deep breath. Imagine a blue and golden light descending over your head, illuminating your mind with creative ideas. Visualize your creativity expanding, generating innovative and brilliant concepts.

## 5. Closing the ritual:

1. Thank the universe for the creative energy received.

2. Write the affirmation: "I am an infinite source of creativity and inspiration. Everything I imagine, I can manifest." and place it in your workspace or study area.

3. Let the candles burn out (or extinguish them with your fingers if you plan to repeat the ritual over several nights).

4. Carry the citrine or lapis lazuli with you as an amulet of creativity and inspiration.

## 6. Duration:

The effects may be felt in the following days with an increase in creative ideas, mental flow, and confidence in artistic expression. You can repeat the ritual during each waxing or full moon to reinforce its power.

## 7. Extra tip:

Before working on creative projects, touch your amulet and repeat: "I am a channel of creativity, ideas flow freely through me."

# 9
# BEAUTY AND ATTRACTIVENESS

# 9.1

## Spell for Personal Charm

THE EMPRESS

## 1. Purpose:

This spell is designed to enhance charisma, natural attraction, and self-confidence, helping you stand out socially, romantically, and professionally. It strengthens your personal energy, projecting magnetism, likability, and confidence.

This ritual will help you:

-Increase charisma and personal magnetism
-Boost self-assurance and confidence
-Attract admiration and improve connection with others
-Eliminate blockages that prevent you from radiating charm and confidence

## 2. Optimal Lunar Phase:

-Waxing Moon: To enhance attractiveness and personal radiance
-Full Moon: To maximize magnetism and social impact

## 3. Materials:

-1 red candle (for charisma and passion)
-1 pink candle (for sweetness and personal harmony)
-1 gold candle (for confidence and social projection)
-Cinnamon (to attract attention and admiration)
-Rose petals (for harmony and energetic beauty)
-Basil (for good luck in relationships and attraction)
-Jasmine oil (for personal magnetism)
-Sandalwood oil (for self-assurance and confidence)
-Rose quartz (for attraction and loving energy)

-Pyrite (for confidence and personal security)
-Tiger's eye (for charisma and determination)
-Tarot card: The Star (for radiance and natural attraction)
-Tarot card: The Sun (for confidence and radiant energy)
-Tarot card: The Empress (for charm, beauty, and sensuality)

## 4. Procedure:

1. Find a quiet place where you can perform the ritual without interruptions. Light jasmine or sandalwood incense to raise the energy and activate personal magnetism.

2. Anoint the red candle with jasmine oil, visualizing your charisma and magnetism activating. Anoint the pink candle with sandalwood oil, feeling your charm increase with harmony. Anoint the gold candle with both oils, ensuring self-confidence and inner security. Sprinkle cinnamon, rose petals, and basil around the candles. Place the rose quartz, pyrite, and tiger's eye near the candles.

3. In the center, place The Star (to attract admiration and charm). On the left, place The Sun (to radiate confidence and security). On the right, place The Empress (to enhance attraction and personal beauty).

4. First, light the red candle, saying: "The fire of my charisma is lit, all eyes turn to me with admiration." Then light the pink candle, saying: "My charm is natural, I attract with sweetness and magnetism." Finally, light the gold candle, saying: "My confidence shines, my presence is powerful."

5. With your hands over the tarot cards and your eyes on the candle flames, repeat with conviction: "Like the moon lights up the night, my charm shines with radiant light." My voice, my laughter, my essence resonate—I attract with grace and leave a lasting impression. The sun gives me strength, the star guides me, my charisma grows, my light shines bright. I am charm, I am beauty, I am power—the world sees me and wants to know me. So it is, so it shall be."

6. Close your eyes and take a deep breath. Imagine a golden light surrounding you, filling you with magnetism and confidence. Visualize people reacting positively to you, admiring your presence and charisma.

## 5. Closing the ritual:

1. Thank the universe for the energy received.

2. Write the affirmation: "My charm is irresistible, my energy is magnetic, my confidence is unshakable." and keep it in your bag or on your personal mirror.

3. Let the candles burn out (or extinguish them with your fingers if you plan to repeat the ritual over several nights).

4. Carry rose quartz or tiger's eye with you as a personal charm amulet.

## 6. Duration:

The effects may be felt in the following days with increased confidence, smoother interactions, and more attention and recognition in your surroundings. You can repeat the ritual during each waxing or full moon to reinforce its power.

## 7. Extra tip:

Before going to an event or important interaction, touch your amulet and repeat: "I am light, I am charm, my presence leaves a mark."

# 9.2

**Spell for Youth and Rejuvenation**

THE EMPRESS

## 1. Purpose:

This spell is designed to revitalize personal energy, slow the signs of aging, and strengthen physical, mental, and spiritual well-being. It helps restore vitality, promote inner balance, and enhance natural beauty from within.

This ritual will help you:

-Revitalize the body, mind, and spirit
-Boost cellular regeneration and energetic youthfulness
-Increase vitality, freshness, and positive energy
-Reinforce confidence and natural beauty

## 2. Optimal Lunar Phase:

-Waxing Moon: To enhance growth and regeneration
-Full Moon: To maximize vital energy and personal radiance

## 3. Materials:

-1 white candle (for purity and renewal)
-1 pink candle (for beauty and harmony)
-1 green candle (for health and vitality)
-Rosemary (for youthfulness and memory)
-Mint (for refreshing and revitalizing energy)
-Rose petals (for beauty and rejuvenation)
-Almond oil (for hydration and regeneration)
-Lavender oil (for peace and energetic harmony)
-Rose quartz (for beauty and self-love)
-Amethyst (for regeneration and balance)
-Jade (for youth and energetic renewal)
-Tarot card: The Empress (for beauty, vitality, and femininity)

-Tarot card: The Sun (for radiant energy and youthfulness)
-Tarot card: The Star (for regeneration and freshness)

## 4. Procedure:

1. Find a quiet place and light lavender or mint incense to harmonize the energy. Place a mirror on the altar to reflect your rejuvenated image.

2. Anoint the white candle with almond oil, visualizing your body being purified and rejuvenated. Anoint the pink candle with lavender oil, feeling harmony and beauty flowing through you. Anoint the green candle with both oils, ensuring health and vitality. Sprinkle rosemary, mint, and rose petals around the candles. Place the rose quartz, amethyst, and jade near the candles.

3. In the center, place The Empress (for beauty and regeneration). On the left, place The Sun (for radiant energy and vitality). On the right, place The Star (for renewal and freshness).

4. First, light the white candle, saying: "The light of youth shines within me, each day my energy is renewed." Then light the pink candle, saying: "My skin glows, my spirit is fresh and radiant." Finally, light the green candle, saying: "My body is strong, my vitality expands with love."

5. With your hands over the tarot cards and your eyes on the candle flames, repeat with conviction: "By the power of the Sun, by the strength of water, my body, my soul, and my essence are renewed." Youth is my ally, energy guides me, my skin glows, my spirit blossoms, my essence vibrates. Time does not rule me, beauty is my reflection, each day I am stronger, younger, more radiant. The light of the moon and the sun bless me, my spirit is eternal, my energy infinite. So it is, so it shall be."

6. Close your eyes and take a deep breath. Imagine a golden

light wrapping around your skin, renewing it and giving it freshness. Visualize your body filled with energy and vitality, feeling rejuvenated.

## 5. Closing the ritual:

1. Thank the universe for the energy of youth and well-being received.

2. Write the affirmation: "My body, my mind, and my spirit are strong, healthy, and full of vitality." and place it on your mirror or in your personal space.

3. Let the candles burn out (or extinguish them with your fingers if you plan to repeat the ritual over several nights).

4. Carry rose quartz or jade with you as an amulet of youth and freshness.

## 6. Duration:

The effects may be felt in the following days with a greater sense of energy, well-being, and rejuvenation. You can repeat the ritual during each waxing or full moon to reinforce its power.

## 7. Extra tip:

Each morning, in front of the mirror, touch your amulet and repeat: "I am vital, youthful, and radiant. My energy renews itself every day."

# 9.3

### Spell for Strong and Shiny Hair

THE EMPRESS

## 1. Purpose:

This spell is designed to strengthen the hair, improve its growth, add shine, and protect it from damage. It also harmonizes personal energy, promoting confidence and beauty from within.

This ritual will help you:

-Strengthen your hair and stimulate growth
-Increase natural shine and softness
-Protect your hair from energetic and environmental damage
-Enhance personal beauty and confidence

## 2. Optimal Lunar Phase:

-Waxing Moon: To stimulate growth and strengthen hair
-Full Moon: To enhance beauty, shine, and hair vitality

## 3. Materials:

-1 green candle (for health and hair growth)
-1 gold candle (for shine and beauty)
-1 white candle (for purification and energetic harmony)
-Rosemary (to strengthen hair and stimulate growth)
-Chamomile (for softness and shine)
-Bay leaf (for protection and hair regeneration)
-Coconut oil (for hydration and hair strengthening)
-Almond oil (for shine and softness)
-Rose quartz (for beauty and self-love)
-Amethyst (for hair harmonization and energetic balance)
-Jade (for strength and hair regeneration)

-Tarot card: The Empress (for beauty, femininity, and hair abundance)
-Tarot card: The Sun (for vitality and hair shine)
-Tarot card: The World (for wholeness and balance in appearance)

## 4. Procedure:

1. Find a quiet place and light chamomile or lavender incense to harmonize the energy. Place a mirror in front of you to visualize your hair full of health and shine.

2. Anoint the green candle with coconut oil, visualizing your hair becoming stronger. Anoint the gold candle with almond oil, feeling your hair shine and become silky. Anoint the white candle with both oils, ensuring protection and energetic harmony. Sprinkle rosemary, chamomile, and bay leaf around the candles. Place the rose quartz, amethyst, and jade near the candles.

3. In the center, place The Empress (to enhance beauty and hair regeneration). On the left, place The Sun (to activate vital energy and hair shine). On the right, place The World (for balance and perfection in personal appearance).

4. First, light the green candle, saying: "My hair is strong, healthy, and abundant." Then light the gold candle, saying: "Shine and softness surround every strand of my hair." Finally, light the white candle, saying: "I am protected, my hair is beautiful and vibrant."

5. With your hands over the tarot cards and your eyes on the candle flames, repeat with conviction: "The strength of the earth nourishes my being, my hair blooms, it is reborn again. I shine like the sun, soft like the wind, my hair is healthy, strong, and beautiful. Water cleanses it, the moon cares for it, the light blesses it, its essence guides me. Each day more beautiful, each day stronger, this is how it remains, this is how it will always be. So it is, so it shall be."

6. Close your eyes and take a deep breath. Imagine a golden light surrounding your hair, filling it with strength and shine. Visualize your hair regenerating, becoming healthier and more beautiful with each moment.

## 5. Closing the ritual:

1. Thank the universe for the energy received.

2. Write the affirmation: "My hair is strong, radiant, and full of life." and place it on your personal mirror.

3. Let the candles burn out (or extinguish them with your fingers if you plan to repeat the ritual over several nights).

4. Carry rose quartz or jade with you as an amulet for beauty and hair health.

## 6. Duration:

The effects may be felt in the following days with a greater sense of hair wellness and self-esteem. You can repeat the ritual during each waxing or full moon to reinforce its power.

## 7. Extra tip:

Before brushing or washing your hair, touch your amulet and repeat: "My hair is my crown, it shines with health and beauty."

# 9.4

## Spell for Radiant Skin

THE EMPRESS

### 1. Purpose:

This spell is designed to enhance the energy of the skin, promoting luminosity, health, and freshness. It works not only on the physical level but also on the energetic, helping you project an image of beauty and harmony from within.

This ritual will help you:

-Improve the health and natural glow of your skin
-Eliminate impurities and balance the energy of the face and body
-Boost self-confidence and inner beauty
-Regenerate and revitalize the skin for a youthful and fresh appearance

### 2. Optimal Lunar Phase:

-Waxing Moon: To enhance regeneration and skin radiance
-Full Moon: To maximize beauty, freshness, and natural facial glow

### 3. Materials:

-1 white candle (for purity and regeneration)
-1 pink candle (for beauty and harmony)
-1 gold candle (for radiance and vibrant energy)
-Chamomile (to soothe and soften the skin)
-Rosemary (for regeneration and glow)
-Lavender (for purification and balance)
-Coconut oil (for hydration and softness)
-Rosehip oil (for cellular regeneration)
-Rose quartz (for beauty and self-love)

-Amethyst (for purification and skin balance)
-Jade (for regeneration and freshness)
-Tarot card: The Empress (for beauty and rejuvenation)
-Tarot card: The Star (for light and radiant skin)
-Tarot card: The Sun (for energy, brightness, and vitality)

## 4. Procedure:

1. Find a quiet place and light lavender or chamomile incense to harmonize the energy. Place a mirror on the altar to visualize your radiant skin.

2. Anoint the white candle with coconut oil, visualizing your skin being purified and rejuvenated. Anoint the pink candle with rosehip oil, feeling your skin becoming soft and glowing. Anoint the gold candle with both oils, ensuring a healthy, natural glow. Sprinkle chamomile, rosemary, and lavender around the candles. Place the rose quartz, amethyst, and jade near the candles.

3. In the center, place The Empress (to enhance beauty and regeneration). On the left, place The Star (for light and skin radiance). On the right, place The Sun (for vitality and radiant energy).

4. First, light the white candle, saying: "My skin is renewed, purified, and filled with light." Then light the pink candle, saying: "My beauty blossoms, my skin glows in harmony." Finally, light the gold candle, saying: "Divine radiance illuminates my skin, my essence is radiant."

5. With your hands over the tarot cards and your eyes on the candle flames, repeat with conviction: "Like dew kisses the flower at dawn, my skin shines with freshness and calm. The moon cares for it, the sun blesses it, my beauty is reborn, my energy glows. The star lights up my skin and soul, my inner light can be seen whole." Radiant, fresh, and healthy—this is my skin, soft and unbreakable. So it is, so it shall be."

6. Close your eyes and take a deep breath. Imagine a golden light descending over your skin, filling it with freshness and luminosity. Visualize your skin regenerating, clearing away impurities, and becoming increasingly healthy and radiant.

## 5. Closing the ritual:

1. Thank the universe for the beauty and well-being energy received.

2. Write the affirmation: "My skin is soft, radiant, and full of life." and place it on your personal mirror.

3. Let the candles burn out (or extinguish them with your fingers if you plan to repeat the ritual over several nights).

4. Carry rose quartz or jade with you as an amulet of beauty and well-being.

## 6. Duration:

The effects may be felt in the following days with a greater sense of well-being, freshness, and skin radiance. You can repeat the ritual during each waxing or full moon to reinforce its power.

## 7. Extra tip:

Before your skincare routine, touch your amulet and repeat: "My skin is luminous, radiant, and full of life."

# 9.5

## Spell for Aesthetic Body Enhancement

THE EMPRESS

## 1. Purpose:

This spell is designed to enhance the beauty and firmness of the body, promote confidence, and help manifest physical changes in a harmonious way. It focuses on energizing the body, strengthening tissues, and improving overall appearance through the connection between mind and energy.

This ritual will help you:

-Promote firmness and toning of the body (breasts, glutes, or any other area you wish)
-Enhance natural beauty and self-confidence
-Manifest desired physical changes with harmony and balance
-Reinforce self-love and confidence in your body image

## 2. Optimal Lunar Phase:

-Waxing Moon: To increase volume, firmness, and growth in desired areas
-Full Moon: To boost harmony, attraction, and overall body beauty

## 3. Materials:

-1 pink candle (for beauty and femininity)
-1 gold candle (for attractiveness and confidence)
-1 green candle (for health and cellular regeneration)
-Fenugreek (known for its properties in enhancing and toning the breasts and glutes)
-Rosemary (for skin regeneration and firmness)

-Cinnamon (to activate circulation and promote physical changes)
-Rosehip oil (for skin elasticity and firmness)
-Almond oil (for nourishment and softness)
-Rose quartz (for femininity and self-love)
-Jade (for regeneration and body toning)
-Amethyst (for bodily harmony and balance)
-Tarot card: The Empress (for beauty, femininity, and bodily abundance)
-Tarot card: The Sun (for radiant energy and physical vitality)
-Tarot card: The World (for physical perfection and balance)

## 4. Procedure:

1. Find a quiet place where you can perform the ritual without interruptions. Light rose or sandalwood incense to raise the energy and enhance femininity. Place a mirror in front of you to visualize the changes you desire in your body.

2. Anoint the pink candle with rosehip oil, visualizing beauty and firmness in your body. Anoint the gold candle with almond oil, feeling your confidence rise. Anoint the green candle with both oils, ensuring health and regeneration. Sprinkle fenugreek, rosemary, and cinnamon around the candles. Place the rose quartz, jade, and amethyst near the candles.

3. In the center, place The Empress (to enhance femininity and body transformation). On the left, place The Sun (to activate vitality and physical manifestation). On the right, place The World (to harmonize and balance the results in the body).

4. First, light the pink candle, saying: "Beauty and harmony flow within me, my body is a temple of love." Then light the gold candle, saying: "My confidence and femininity expand, my attractiveness shines." Finally, light the green candle, saying: "My skin, my curves, and my energy are renewed and strengthened."

5. With your hands over the tarot cards and your eyes on the candle flames, repeat with conviction: "The moon guides me, the earth nourishes me, my body responds, my beauty flows. Every cell glows, every curve lifts according to my desires, my skin tightens, my essence renews. The Empress blesses me, the Sun illuminates me, my body is perfect, my energy divine. I am strong, I am beautiful, my confidence blossoms, my image expands, my being radiates. So it is, so it shall be."

6. Close your eyes and take a deep breath. Imagine a golden and pink light flowing through your body, firming and harmonizing every part. Visualize your breasts, glutes, or any area you wish to enhance becoming more toned, firm, healthy, and reaching the desired volume and shape.

## 5. Closing the ritual:

1. Thank the universe for the energy received.

2. Write the affirmation: "My body is firm, beautiful, and harmonious. Each day it improves and radiates." Place it on your mirror or in your personal care area.

3. Let the candles burn out (or extinguish them with your fingers if you plan to repeat the ritual over several nights).

4. Carry rose quartz or jade with you as an amulet of beauty and body firmness.

## 6. Duration:

The effects may be felt in the following days with an increased sense of confidence, firmness, and well-being in the body. You can repeat the ritual during each waxing or full moon to reinforce its power.

## 7. Extra tip:

Before exercising or applying firming creams, touch your

amulet and repeat: "My body is firm, beautiful, and strong—each day it improves and transforms."

# 9.6

**Spell for Magnetic Attraction**

III
THE EMPRESS

## 1. Purpose:

This spell is designed to enhance your personal magnetism, making you more attractive in social, romantic, and professional settings. It strengthens the energy of charisma, presence, and confidence, helping you naturally attract attention and admiration.

This ritual will help you:

-Boost personal magnetism and natural attraction
-Increase charisma and self-confidence
-Improve connection with others and draw attention
-Release insecurities and project seductive energy

## 2. Optimal Lunar Phase:

-Waxing Moon: To enhance charisma and attraction
-Full Moon: To maximize magnetism and personal presence

## 3. Materials:

-1 red candle (for desire and attraction)
-1 pink candle (for sweetness and personal charm)
-1 gold candle (for confidence and inner glow)
-Cinnamon (for magnetism and personal appeal)
-Rose petals (for sweetness and natural attraction)
-Ginger (for energy and seduction)
-Jasmine oil (to enhance magnetism and sensuality)
-Sandalwood oil (for confidence and charisma)
-Rose quartz (for romantic attraction and sweetness)
-Pyrite (for confidence and magnetic attraction)

-Tiger's eye (for personal security and charisma)
-Tarot card: The Star (to radiate magnetism and admiration)
-Tarot card: The Sun (for luminous and charismatic presence)
-Tarot card: The Empress (to enhance beauty and natural attraction)

## 4. Procedure:

1. Find a quiet place and light jasmine or cinnamon incense to raise the energy. Place a mirror near the altar to visualize yourself with magnetism and confidence.

2. Anoint the red candle with jasmine oil, visualizing your magnetism and desire awakening. Anoint the pink candle with sandalwood oil, feeling your natural charm being amplified. Anoint the gold candle with both oils, ensuring self-assurance and confidence. Sprinkle cinnamon, rose petals, and ginger around the candles. Place the rose quartz, pyrite, and tiger's eye near the candles.

3. In the center, place The Star (to attract admiration and charm). On the left, place The Sun (to radiate confidence and security). On the right, place The Empress (to boost beauty and personal magnetism).

4. First, light the red candle, saying: "The fire within me awakens, my attraction shines." Then light the pink candle, saying: "My charm is natural, my energy is irresistible." Finally, light the gold candle, saying: "My confidence glows, my magnetism draws with power."

5. With your hands over the tarot cards and your eyes on the candle flames, repeat with conviction: "As the moon draws the tides, as the sun lights up the days, so does my presence shine and enchant, my magnetism captivates, my essence leaves its mark." My energy is powerful, my light is strong, I attract with grace, with passion and luck. Whoever sees me will remember me, whoever feels me will long for me. So it is, so it shall be.

6. Close your eyes and take a deep breath. Imagine a golden and pink light expanding from your chest, surrounding you in an aura of irresistible magnetism. Visualize people reacting positively to you, feeling drawn to your energy and charisma.

## 5. Closing the ritual:

1. Thank the universe for the energy received.

2. Write the affirmation: "I am light, I am charm, my magnetism is irresistible." Keep it in your bag or on your personal mirror.

3. Let the candles burn out (or extinguish them with your fingers if you plan to repeat the ritual over several nights).

4. Carry tiger's eye or pyrite with you as an amulet of personal attraction.

## 6. Duration:

The effects may be felt in the following days with increased confidence, smoother interactions, and stronger attraction toward you. You can repeat the ritual during each waxing or full moon to reinforce its power.

## 7. Extra tip:

Before going to an event or important interaction, touch your amulet and repeat: "My energy shines, my presence attracts, my magnetism leaves a mark."

# 9.7

## Spell to Achieve Ideal Weight

THE EMPRESS

## 1. Purpose:

This spell is designed to balance the body and mind, helping you naturally reach and maintain a healthy weight. It aligns your bodily energy with your desired goal, promotes positive habits, and dissolves emotional blockages that may affect metabolism and eating behaviors.

This ritual will help you:

-Support a balanced metabolism and digestion
-Eliminate emotional blockages that hinder weight control
-Increase discipline and motivation for healthy habits
-Promote harmony between body and mind

## 2. Optimal Lunar Phase:

-Waning Moon: To eliminate excess weight and cleanse the body
-Waxing Moon: To strengthen metabolism and attract healthy habits

## 3. Materials:

-1 green candle (for health and balance)
-1 blue candle (for mental peace and emotional control)
-1 white candle (for purification and transformation)
-Mint (to boost metabolism and digestion)
-Ginger (to burn fat and increase energy)
-Bay leaf (for willpower and discipline)
-Lemon oil (for cleansing and mental clarity)
-Rosemary oil (for energy and circulation)
-Amethyst (to control anxiety and cravings)

-Citrine (for metabolism and willpower)
-Green quartz (for health and overall well-being)
-Tarot card: Temperance (for balance and self-control)
-Tarot card: The Chariot (for progress and determination)
-Tarot card: The Star (for confidence and self-satisfaction)

## 4. Procedure:

1. Find a quiet place and light rosemary or mint incense to harmonize the energy. Keep a glass of lemon water nearby as a symbol of purification.

2. Anoint the green candle with lemon oil, visualizing your body aligning with your ideal weight. Anoint the blue candle with rosemary oil, feeling your mind align with healthy habits. Anoint the white candle with both oils, ensuring energetic cleansing and transformation. Sprinkle mint, ginger, and bay leaf around the candles. Place the amethyst, citrine, and green quartz near the candles.

3. In the center, place Temperance (for balance and control over the body and eating). On the left, place The Chariot (for determination and progress toward your goal). On the right, place The Star (to reinforce confidence and self-assurance).

4. First, light the green candle, saying: "My body is balanced, my health is strong." Then light the blue candle, saying: "My mind is calm, my habits align with my well-being." Finally, light the white candle, saying: "My transformation is certain, my body reflects my best self."

5. With your hands over the tarot cards and your eyes on the candle flames, repeat with conviction: "Balance manifests in my body, each day I move forward with certainty. My health blossoms, my energy aligns, my ideal weight reflects my true light. I release the excess, I release the burden, my body transforms, my being advances. I am strong, I am free, my change is real— with love and care, I achieve my ideal. So it is, so it shall be."

6. Close your eyes and take a deep breath. Imagine a green and golden light flowing through your body, balancing your metabolism. Visualize your body healthy, light, and in its ideal form.

## 5. Closing the ritual:

1. Thank the universe for the energy received.

2. Drink the glass of lemon water to seal the cleansing and renewal of your body.

3. Write the affirmation: "My body is healthy, strong, and balanced. Each day I get closer to my ideal weight." and place it on your mirror or in your meditation space.

4. Let the candles burn out (or extinguish them with your fingers if you plan to repeat the ritual over several nights).

5. Carry citrine or amethyst with you as an amulet of balance and willpower.

## 6. Duration:

The effects may be felt in the following days with increased motivation, balance, and healthy habits. You can repeat the ritual during each waning or waxing moon, depending on your goal.

## 7. Extra tip:

Before each meal or workout, touch your amulet and repeat: "My body and mind work together. I am in balance, and my transformation is positive."

# 9.8

## Spell to Release Insecurities About Physical Appearance

THE EMPRESS

### 1. Purpose:

This spell is designed to release emotional blockages related to self-image, increase self-esteem, and help you see your true beauty. It supports confidence and allows you to project an image of self-love and security.

This ritual will help you:

-Eliminate negative thoughts about physical appearance
-Boost self-esteem and self-love
-Develop a positive self-image
-Project confidence and assurance in your own beauty

### 2. Optimal Lunar Phase:

-Waning Moon: To eliminate insecurities and negative thoughts
-Waxing Moon: To strengthen self-esteem and self-love

### 3. Materials:

-1 white candle (for purification and renewal)
-1 pink candle (for self-love and inner beauty)
-1 gold candle (for confidence and security)
-Rose petals (for self-acceptance and natural beauty)
-Lavender (for harmony and inner peace)
-Rosemary (to remove negative energies and strengthen confidence)
-Coconut oil (to nourish self-esteem and personal energy)
-Jasmine oil (to boost confidence and magnetism)
-Rose quartz (for self-love and personal acceptance)

-Amethyst (for peace and the transformation of negative thoughts)
-Tiger's eye (for confidence and self-assurance)
-Tarot card: The Empress (for beauty, self-love, and femininity)
-Tarot card: The Sun (for confidence and self-acceptance)
-Tarot card: The Star (to radiate confidence and personal glow)

## 4. Procedure:

1. Find a quiet place and light lavender or rose incense to harmonize the energy. Place a mirror in front of you to visualize yourself with love and acceptance.

2. Anoint the white candle with coconut oil, visualizing your insecurities dissolving. Anoint the pink candle with jasmine oil, feeling self-love grow within you. Anoint the gold candle with both oils, ensuring confidence and security. Sprinkle rose petals, lavender, and rosemary around the candles. Place the rose quartz, amethyst, and tiger's eye near the candles.

3. In the center, place The Empress (to enhance beauty and self-love). On the left, place The Sun (to strengthen self-esteem and assurance). On the right, place The Star (to radiate confidence and natural attraction).

4. First, light the white candle, saying: "Insecurities and fears disappear, my mind is set free." Then light the pink candle, saying: "I love and accept myself as I am, my beauty is unique." Finally, light the gold candle, saying: "I trust myself, my light shines with confidence and love."

5. With your hands over the tarot cards and your eyes on the candle flames, repeat with conviction: "I look at myself with love, I accept myself without fear, my beauty blossoms, my being is sincere. There is no judgment, no fear, in my reflection I see love. The light of the sun shines upon me,

my confidence guides me. I shine brightly, without doubt
or fear, my essence is strong, my beauty is love.  So it is,
so it shall be."

6. Close your eyes and take a deep breath. Imagine a pink
and golden light surrounding you, dissolving all insecurity.
Visualize your reflection in the mirror with a smile of
confidence and self-love.

**5. Closing the ritual:**

1. Thank the universe for the energy of self-love and
confidence received.

2. Write the affirmation: "I am beautiful just as I am.
My confidence shines and my beauty is unique."
Place it on your mirror or in your personal care area.

3. Let the candles burn out (or extinguish them with your
fingers if you plan to repeat the ritual over several nights).

4. Carry rose quartz or tiger's eye with you as an amulet of
confidence and self-love.

**6. Duration:**

The effects may be felt in the following days with increased
self-esteem, confidence, and assurance in your appearance.
You can repeat the ritual during each waning moon to release
doubts, or during the waxing moon to boost your confidence.

**7. Extra tip:**

Each morning, look at yourself in the mirror and repeat:
"I love and accept myself. My confidence is my greatest
asset, my beauty is unique."

Made in the USA
Coppell, TX
01 July 2025

51374609R00105